THE BEST OF PHILIP HOLDEN

THE BEST OF PHILIP HOLDEN

Hunting lore and back-country yarns

Philip Holden

HarperCollinsPublishers

HarperCollins*Publishers*

The stories in this collection were first published as shown on pages 5–6.
This edition published in 2012
by HarperCollins*Publishers (New Zealand) Limited*
PO Box 1, Shortland Street, Auckland 1140

HarperCollins*Publishers*
31 View Road, Glenfield, Auckland 0627, New Zealand
Level 13, 201 Elizabeth Street, Sydney, NSW 2000, Australia
A 53, Sector 57, Noida, UP, India
77–85 Fulham Palace Road, London W6 8JB, United Kingdom
2 Bloor Street East, 20th floor, Toronto, Ontario M4W 1A8, Canada
10 East 53rd Street, New York, NY 10022, USA

National Library of New Zealand Cataloguing-in-Publication Data

Holden, Philip.
The best of Philip Holden / Philip Holden.
ISBN 978-1-86950-990-3
1. Hunting—New Zealand. I. Title.
799.2993—dc 23

ISBN: 978 1 86950 990 3

Cover and internal design and typesetting by Cheryl Rowe
All photos by Philip Holden unless otherwise indicated

Colour reproduction by Graphic Print Group, South Australia
Printed by RR Donnelley, China, on 128gsm Matt Art

Contents

Introduction

Born in North Wales in 1937, Philip Holden immigrated with his family to Australia in 1953.

After leaving school at the age of 15 he worked in the Australian outback. It was here that he discovered within himself a lasting love of hunting, rifles, horses, and the wild country.

As a young adult it was almost with disbelief that he read of paid positions available as full-time deer cullers within the New Zealand Forest Service. They needed tough men who were self-reliant and, of course, crack shots. And so at the age of 23 he made the move to New Zealand where, apart from some short breaks, he spent seven years as a full-time deer culler. It was at the end of this period that he discovered his passion for writing.

Holden, now with a young wife, felt the need to make a change and tried returning to town life, finally settling in Wellington. Here he worked as a postman, running his daily route in order to free his afternoons which he devoted to writing.

After 20 months away from the hills and with an alluring upturn in the price of venison, Holden moved to Hawke's Bay where he spent a year in the incredibly demanding vocation as a full-time meat shooter.

It was with great success in 1971 that he published his first work, the New Zealand classic *Pack and Rifle*.

Encouraged by his initial success he produced another two popular works, *Hunter by Profession* (1973) and *Backblocks* (1974).

Over the next three decades Holden gained a dedicated following and reputation amongst the rural and outdoor/hunting community of New Zealand and Australia, not just as a narrator of hunting adventures but also as a talented photographer, historian and fictional writer. Works such as *The Deer Hunters* (1976), *The Golden Years of Hunting in New Zealand* (1983), *The Hunting Experience* (1988), *Along the Dingo Fence* (1991), the *Station Country* series (1993, 1995 and 1997) and his young adult fiction, *Fawn* (1976), *Stag* (1980) and *Razorback* (1984), are testament to the range of his ability.

By the end of his life in 2005 he had firmly established himself as one of New Zealand's most prolific authors with over 50 published volumes of work to his credit.

Philip Holden with a trophy rusa stag, 1966.

What does hunting mean to the genuine hunter?

Firstly, there is the sheer thrill of the hunt — the opportunity to pit one's skills and wits against those of the wild whose senses are far keener and whose speed is so much greater …

Hunting in the noblest sense of the meaning is treating one's chosen quarry with the utmost respect. Definitely the days of indiscriminate killing are over. Therefore a genuinely caring hunter — with a long-term view to conserving rather than eliminating that which he hunts — will take only a specific trophy animal of a certain species, or possibly a young beast for meat …

Above all else perhaps,

hunting means doing manly things where the view is uncluttered by man's progress. It means being where the air is clear and good to breathe, and where the water in the creeks and rivers is unpolluted.

— Extracts from a speech given by Philip Holden at the launching of *The Deer Stalkers* in Taupo, July 1987

Big River — Running High

In the gloom of early morning the Arthur River in Fiordland National Park presents a sobering sight after a night of torrential rain.

From Big Hill tent camp we moved up to Ruahine hut on a cold and blustery day, and after the tent camp that hut was sheer heaven. For Ruahine is the latest kind of Forest Service hut: they have six bunks for a start, and each one has a foam-rubber mattress. There's also a verminproof food cupboard, a workbench, and several bins for perishables such as flour, butter, cheese and so on. These huts are spacious, very practical and damn comfortable to live in.

It was now well over two years since I'd been at Dip Flat and by now I'd found out how the back country can grow on a man. At first, when I mused over it, there was no feeling of belonging. In the role of an intruder I'd been too much of a stranger for that. But now I seemed to have blended in — to have become, in a way, a part of it all. And now I was under the spell there was no turning back. Not ever. But while a man can love and feel akin to the remote places, he must never trust or underestimate them, for their ever-treacherous terrain, swift-rising rivers and adverse conditions wait patiently for the unwary.

It must have been only a few degrees above freezing that late July day when I left Ruahine hut to hunt the surrounds of the Ngaruroro River. I hadn't wanted to hunt that way at all, but as it was my last choice … Anyway, as I neared the river, six multicoloured blobs stood out sharp and clear on the greyish, sheer rocky faces across the river. Shooting them presented no problem — but that river did. For the Ngaruroro was a dark brown churning torrent. I wanted those goat tails real bad, for Keith was leading me, tallywise, as he did everyone else, but not by many. Another six and I'd be right behind him — possibly in front, if he missed out today. But that wasn't at all likely.

I squatted down. It was a cheerless spot: the huge rocks on the water's edge were covered with ice and there was a dampish chill in the air. Roll on the spring and summer, I thought. I did a quick reckon up: I hadn't realised it before but those six tails would put me one in front of Keith. Although crossing large rivers has always scared me when they're running high, I decided I'd risk it. I kept my boots and knife belt on, and leaving the rest of my gear on the bank I tentatively moved a few feet into the water, where it was already up to my waist. Get out you bloody mug, cried a warning voice from within. But I tried one more step and the next moment I was knocked off my feet and swept away. It's a fact that until you've been in a similar position you have no idea of the tremendous speed and awesome power that adds up to a back-country river in flood. You haven't a cat in hell's chance of swimming against such a flow so you go with the current and try to angle in towards the bank. And that's what I did until I reached the far side where, after a short rest, I tailed the easy-to-reach goats.

Now I had a problem — because upriver was much worse, and downstream the Ngaruroro narrowed its way through a sheer-faced gorge. Well, you've done it once I told myself, you can do it again. But it was with a feeling of dread that I approached the water. For a long moment I hesitated (that warning voice was insisting again) before edging myself in.

If you can keep your balance in a river that's up, you're not too bad; because going with the current you can sort of leap along — keeping upright and touching the bottom every yard or so. It's the time-honoured way. However, that's all well and good but only when the river's not too deep. Anyway, there's me hopping along in chest-deep water, feeling mighty pleased with myself as the bank was coming close, when suddenly and, following a forward sort of hop, the river closed in over my head. Spluttering water I bobbed up and began to fight my way for land. Or I should have been — because I was putting everything into a kind of dog-paddle and crawl stroke combination. But the previous crossing must have taken all my strength, for I could make no progress, and now the panic came. Several times I was forced under and once, when the river became shallow for a little way, my hip cracked hard against a boulder, and then I was in deep water again.

I know I was more scared than I had ever been. I was being carried along like a mere leaf, and I thought for the first time in my life that I might be killed. Now the river thundered into the gorge that I'd noticed downstream. Then, when it looked as if nothing could save me, the current carried me to the far bank and slammed me against an outcrop of rock.

My hands grabbed for a hold and I managed to hang on. Then bit by bit I managed to drag myself up until I was safe. As I lay there, reaction shook me like a leaf in a gale and when that had passed I made my way upriver to my gear on unsteady legs. The next time I spot goats across the Ngaruroro, I thought, they can bloody well stay there. New Zealand's high-country rivers have claimed the lives of too many government hunters.

Back at the hut, I found out from a smiling Keith that he'd shot four deer. Of all the professionals I've known, Keith Lane, Peter Cook, and Jim Warren, who comes into my story later, were by far the most consistent hunters. It was a rare day indeed when any of them missed out. Magnificent hunters all. I wish that I'd been as good.

Fallow deer bucks in late May. They are running together in the aftermath of the rutting season. The bucks on the extreme left and right are top trophies, whereas the middle one's antlers lack palmation.

A week later I was in the same place and blow me if there weren't six more goats across the river. Not quite in the same place, but several hundred yards further upstream this time. The river was still well up, though; the days of snow and sleet and steady rain had made sure of that. I decided to shoot them and return when the river dropped. My present spot was not the place to shoot from, though,

A cool spring dawn, looking over Lake Rotoiti towards the St Arnaud Range.

because here I needed both hands to hang on to a steep rock and clay hill-face. Taking it easy I reached a wide ledge and from here all that could be heard was the turbulent waters of the Ngaruroro. From the sitting position I lined up the 7 x 57 and settled the 4x Pecar scope onto a bulky, slate-grey billy. Poised on an out-thrusting rock with his heavy black horns twisted back he was an impressive sight as the breeze that came up from the river ruffled his long and matted black mane. Feeding close to the old boy and scattered over a small radius were the other five. I took that proud billy with a chest shot and he came bouncing limply down to jam behind a rock. Following the shot there was a bewildered, shocked response from the others, and one by one they fell, the last one almost reaching the water's edge.

Two days passed and, as there had been no more rain, I went back to the river. Those two days had made a great difference and now around its normal height, the Ngaruroro flowed almost sluggishly. Fording wasn't difficult, but I took it carefully, for she was still dirty and the riverbed was mainly slime-covered rocks. Shivering, I came out on the far side, shook myself like a dog, then tailed the water's-edge goat and began to climb for the rest. The stiffened billy, with horns that would have spanned a good thirty inches, was easily retrieved, and one of the others was also easy to reach. The remaining three — now here was something different. To tail these meant a trip across a narrow, very steep face of loose rock, clay, and small tenacious bits of scrubby growth and clumps of coarse grass. Below was a drop of at least eighty feet to the rocks, give or take an inch.

While not liking the look of what lay ahead before I began, it was frankly nothing to the feeling that overcame me about halfway. Suddenly my legs had a mind of their own: they simply refused to go. What the hell are you doing here, I thought, risking your damn fool neck for three lousy goat tails? Then the bit of scrub that I was grasping with my right hand did a remarkably stupid thing — it gave a little at the roots, and the narrow ledge I stood on slowly began to crumble. I looked down — make that ninety feet above the river. Action was called for but I had no choice, as my eleven and a half stone abruptly proved too much for that bit of scrub, and there above the rocks I did a sideways leap that would have done credit to a chamois. Well, how about a goat? My leap for life ended up with me hanging by both arms to a growth known as leatherwood. Now all I had to do was to swing back, then forward, and let go. Which I did, landing in a sprawling but relieved heap on top of one of the goats. And there I rested until the sick feeling in my stomach had passed.

The winter dragged on. We covered the block and stayed at all the huts except for those on the main range, because of deep snow up there. From Ruahine to Dead Dog — now that's a name for you — and from there to Herrick's Base, to Sentry Box, and back round again. Four men who always seemed to be wet, never quite relaxed in each other's company and prone to bitch over the slightest thing. Four men who had simply had more than a gutful of living in one room with three others. Then towards the end of September, and at a time when things were more than a little strained, the four-man party was suddenly no more. Keith Lane was transferred to the western Ruahines, with hardly any warning; Leo Smith decided to hunt the block on his own, which proved that he had initiative; and Barry Hunt and

myself hutted together. It was wonderful to be in a two-man party again. Lean, very dry-humoured Barry Hunt is five feet eleven of damn good company. And, best of all, he never takes himself seriously.

So we were at Ruahine hut once more, Barry and I. The snow flurried endlessly about the door and both of us were planning ways of spending the two-week September break which was due soon. In those days and in the Wellington Conservancy only, the hunters had three two-week spells spread over the year: at Christmas, early in May, and the one that was coming up now. You needed them.

Anyway, when Barry suggested that we spend our last week or so at No Mans hut I was up and packing my gear. The walk to No Mans is normally an easy two hours along the bare tops, but not when the snow is deep and still falling. With his cheeks stung red by a wind that whipped off the snow and was winter itself, Barry battled along, and over his shoulder told me that there used to be a hunter

The old and the new. On the left is a Winchester Model 1895 in .303 British calibre, and today's Sako .25-06.

on this block who, when walking between huts, had his transistor radio tuned in loudly to 2ZC Hawke's Bay. I laughed at that one. Music to pack by — what next?

Eventually — three hours after leaving, and to our frozen relief — the blurred outline of No Mans hut came into view. The snow was to keep up for the rest of the day. But that didn't worry either of us, no sir; the hut was well stocked with food, the radio reception was first rate, and the roaring fire soon warmed the entire hut, which is unusual for a camp at this height (4290 feet) in such weather.

That night I climbed out of my bag, went outside and moved well away from the hut. It was almost unreal outside, with a hard, bright moon reflecting on the crisp snow.

I returned to find the door locked. Hunt, the bastard, I thought. Well, two can play games, can't they? So moving a little way from the door I crouched down behind a low bush. Apart from my tennis shoes I wore nothing, so waiting for the enemy to show was, like, cool. Ten minutes passed and there'd been no noise from inside. Then the door opened

a little way and a candlelit head poked ever so cautiously around the door post.

'Come on in, Phil,' he called out. Then, 'You must be freezing out there!'

I didn't reply, but patiently waited until more of Barry was exposed. When he was fully in sight and again called, 'Come in, Phil', I let him have it with a large, juicy snowball. Barry was not dressed for visitors either and that large, juicy snowball connected in the locality of his most tender spot.

'You rotten sod,' he yelled, charging forth. But I was ready, and from my large heap of snowballs I bombed him. He cursed and retreated out of range, where he rapidly commenced to make his own ammo. For a while, warfare raged at 2 a.m. in the high Ruahines.

'Truce, truce,' I finally cried, for by now I was numb with cold, and besides, Barry was winning this battle.

'Right,' Barry yelled. 'Truce', flinging a final well-aimed snowball at me before racing back to the hut.

Barry was one hell of a good man to be teamed up with.

Pack and Rifle — 1971

The Way It Is

A 'rare' white fallow buck during the mating season. The two
younger animals — spikers — act in a watchdog capacity and,
like the does, warn the master buck of danger.

My trip overseas lasted seven months. I went back to Wales and visited the house where I had spent the greater part of my first fifteen years. But the big field that faced my old home, where the grass grew at least five feet high in the summer and where in season the blackberry and raspberry bushes would be heavy with fruit, and where we used to play cricket and soccer and build a great bonfire on November the fifth, was now covered with houses. That, I think, depressed me more than anything had in a long while.

By the time the SS *Southern Cross* reached Wellington on the return trip in January '65 I was able, but only just, to buy myself a rail ticket to Auckland.

While in London I'd got in touch with Norm Gilmore and he had come good at my request for a job. I didn't know where I'd be sent, but that in itself mattered little. Just to be a professional hunter again would be more than enough for me.

Six days after arriving back I flew into Napier, with the help of NAC. It was a fine sunny day, and when I remember all the times I've visited Napier, the sun always seems to be shining. Anyway (after that small plug for Hawke's Bay), I bowled into the Forestry office where Norm sat smiling behind a big desk; and Morrie Robson likewise, on the edge of it.

'Chuck your gear in the back of my Bedford,' said Morrie after a few pleasantries. 'You're coming back to Kuripapango with me.'

So began my second stint in the Kawekas.

I spent the first three weeks back roaming the high country with Darryl Steele, and the days passed quickly. During my absence the lucrative overseas venison industry had really swung into top gear. Remote South Island valleys that had known only an infrequent visitor in the past, now began to regularly hear the mechanical clatter of the aerial meat-shooters; riflemen in jetboats were now hunting the surrounds of the big waterways of both islands, and anywhere accessible to a vehicle was spotlighted relentlessly; and the likes of me were still hammering away at blocks that had been shot for years. And apart from all this professional activity there seemed to be more and more private hunters invading the hills. (And why not? That's what I'd be doing every weekend if it were not my living …)

So as I left Darryl at Studholmes Saddle hut to spend the last week or so on my own, the pressure, more than ever, was really on the deer.

A damp clinging mist was down that day and a biting icy wind lashed as I crossed the main Kaweka Range at around the 5000-foot mark. To many, I suppose, a Forestry hut doesn't look up to much — but when you've been travelling for a couple of hours in lousy conditions, a Forestry hut means a lot to a hunter. Back Ridge hut, as I neared it on that summer's day with hands that ached because they were so cold and a face that was numb and stiff from the wind, looked like a Hilton hotel to me.

The following morning the weather was still bad, but in the early afternoon, when I was contemplating making another batch of fried scones, even though I could hardly fasten my shorts, the man in charge of things up there suddenly decided that as a fine day had been forecast for the area he'd better do something about it … So the grey was swept away as well as the rain, and the wind that had been buffeting the hut abruptly ran out of steam. Standing in the doorway I decided to have a look at the bivvy on Back Ridge itself.

Back Ridge is, for the main part, a shark's-fin of a ridge. South from the bivvy, which is an hour's walk from Back Ridge hut, the country was during all my time in the Kawekas a great hunting ground. I don't doubt for one moment that it's any different now. When I reached the large, sloping clearing where the bivvy stands, there wasn't much light left. I'd purposely left it late in the hope of picking up handy meat, for the clearing was always a likely spot when no one had been around for a while.

That evening there was a nice plump yearling feeding no more than fifty yards from the bivvy. Handy meat, all right. I took one back leg and also the liver and kidneys, then dragged the much lighter carcass further away from camp. There are more than enough flies around in the hot months without encouraging them. There were several tins of pepper in the bivvy, so I sprinkled a good covering over the exposed parts of the meat and then scaled a handy tree to its topmost branches. The pepper dries the meat quickly, and the height helps to keep the flies away. (Another way to beat the flies is to submerge the meat in water. Although it turns white, it's still okay.)

This bivvy is around five feet high by seven feet long; at one end is a door and facing that a small window; add a couple of mattresses as well as a small kerosene cooker and that's your lot, mate. A bivvy like this is quite good to camp in for a few days if the weather's good and you don't mind stooping about all the time. There wasn't much to eat — but I'd expected that; I'd brought myself some rice and a little coffee. It was enough.

After sorting things out, putting some water on to boil

A red deer hind with her offspring.

*Two adult red deer hinds and their offspring meandering down a
swollen stream on Te Awaiti Station, Wairarapa.*

and fixing up the radio aerial, I set about making one of my
favourite meals. To start with, the two handfuls of long-grain
rice went into boiling, salted water for fifteen minutes, no
more, no less, then I strained it and spread it evenly over
the camp-oven lid as there were no plates. In the meantime
I had semi-grilled thin slices of liver and kidney in the
camp oven, using only a mere trace of lard. I'd kept a good
watch on them too, as they cook in no time. The liver and
kidney were now spread over the rice and I'd come across
a bottle of Worcester sauce, so I gave the dish a liberal dose;
when this mixes with the juices from the meat and soaks
throughout the rice, it's very fair tucker for a hungry man.

It was chilly the following morning, but obviously a fine
day was on the agenda as I angled up from the bivvy and
headed south along the ridge-top. I knew I was going to see
deer. Call it intuition, call it hunter's instinct, call it what you
like, but when you get that feeling then you're going to see
deer. After about thirty minutes, long green, grassy guts and
open, bare faces began to sweep up from the bush-edge to
the ridge-top on both sides. Here, on the Kiwi Creek side,
I spotted five deer. I crouched down quickly as up to that
moment I'd been foolishly on the skyline. I could have shot
from my present spot as the deer were less than a hundred
yards away, but against that was the angle of the shot, never
easy shooting downhill; and the fact that they were only a
few bounds away from the trees. In this game you get close
and, if it's possible, closer still.

By moving a little further away and then by dropping
down a clay gut I got to within thirty yards or so. When I'd
begun my short stalk, my final sight of the deer had been
of them all feeding, but now as I raised a cautious head up
from the clay gut, every one of them was looking directly at
me. Damn! At a moment like this you act quickly — and, if

you can, shoot a hind first — they're the smart ones in any bunch of red deer. As one of the two hinds was head on I took her with a chest shot. I reloaded as she went down but the others had already spun around and raced for cover. Just too late for a second shot. One out of five, I mused, as I tailed the hind: not good enough, boy.

Climbing back to the ridge I discovered in a small saucer-shaped hollow that while there had been no professional activity on Back Ridge of late, others had been around: four stags lay stiff and still in that small radius: four stags that had not been touched in any way whatsoever.

I rarely get mad, but I was mad then. Now it's all right with me to be a hunter in the Forest Service, naturally, for while you only take a tail from a kill, it's what you are paid for. Right? It's okay with me, too, if you shoot for meat. While many claim that meat-shooters are much too mercenary, I disagree. I reckon that anyone who carries out a deer in this up-and-down country is entitled to whatever he can get for it, and good luck to him. It's fine with me also to shoot for trophies — be it antlers or skins. And I do admire the straight-out trophy-shooter. What I do object to is to kill for no gain whatsoever, and the person or persons who had accounted for these stags had done just that. I hate this kind of shooter and the type that leaves bullet-shattered beer bottles along the roadside, or a signpost full of holes; and sometimes, because the hunting has been poor, his frustration will run to shooting livestock. Little wonder, then, that so many property owners, who are damn touchy to start with, now won't allow any shooters on their land. Just a few spoil it for the rest.

I looked at the stags once more. Two of them had a large rack of velvet and in 1965 that was worth a few quid. But nothing had been taken, not even a single backsteak.

The Ruger Model-77 with 3x Lyman scope which Philip Holden used on his return to the Kaweka Mountains.

Pack and Rifle — 1971

Time of the Roar

The roar. A time of waiting, as taut as a bowstring while a maddened stag plunges noisily but unseen through the scrub towards you. Of the hope that the bellowing beast over the next ridge will be a real trophy. The one you've looked for and waited for, until one day he's suddenly there.

Yes, the roar is something all right. It's the pick of the hunting year when it all happens, when that first real roar of the season sends a tingle of suppressed excitement coursing through you.

The first roar I ever heard was a sound that drifted up from a misty gully and was, I thought, as much a true cry of the wilderness as anything could be.

The roar is the rutting time of the red deer and it begins slowly, in say late March, and it's then that the stags are in splendid condition after their long, lazy summer. By early May it's just about over, but in between and particularly in mid-April the roar is on in earnest, for by then the stags have gathered their hinds together and more or less settled into a specific piece of territory, and their full-bodied roars, bellows, and deep, long-drawn-out moans tell other stags that this is their piece of country and those hinds belong to them.

Although red stags rarely fight, they will, if sufficiently provoked, engage in combat. These battles, which are seldom seen by man, are fierce, lengthy as a rule, and occasionally end in death.

When the roar is over the stags go their own way. They are tired out and gaunt — the excessive mating and little interest in food have made sure of that. Now they're seeking a secluded place where they can rest up and eat. From the hunter's angle they're hard to locate then, but this is only fair, for over the time of the roar the red stags give the hunter ample opportunities.

For the roar period the Kaweka hunters were away from base for six weeks, and, as the Forest Park covers some 250,000 acres, Ranger Morrie Robson required six men to cover the entire area satisfactorily. At that time he had four regulars: Herb Reihana, Brian Burdon, a crack hunter and fine hut-mate who like me was in the Kawekas for the second time, and Darryl Steele and myself.

Morrie also dropped a line to those Kaweka oldtimers, Geoff Beale and Hank Christensen, and suggested that if they wished and, of course, could fit it in, they were welcome to six weeks on the payroll. Both made it.

As Hank said not long after arriving at the Kaweka base: 'Six weeks of hunting at the very best time of the year? And being paid for it too? I'd be a mug to turn it down!'

So the Kawekas were split into three. Herb and Hank were to cover the pick of the block — the Harkness area; Geoff and Brian the eastern side, where the hunting was hard; and Darryl and I had the Manson and Back Ridge country. Not as good as the Harkness, admittedly, but a whole lot better than the eastern side.

It was early April 1965, and the odd stags had began to roar well, a far cry from their tentative efforts of the week before. Darryl and I had just reached Kiwi Mouth hut on a very warm morning, en route to the Manson lands. To hunt there we would camp in the Manson hut, but to do so meant that we'd have to take food with us. So that's what we were doing at Kiwi Mouth — picking up supplies.

'How much grub do you reckon we'll need?' Darryl was saying.

'As much as we can carry,' I replied, poking around in the food cupboard. 'I'd like to spend a good week at least on the Manson.'

'But we'll have to come back for more,' said Darryl,

'won't we? What we can carry with us isn't going to last anywhere near a week.'

'It should,' I replied and grinned sharklike at him, 'with plenty of venison.'

And Darryl, whose teeth were giving him trouble, visibly winced.

I've carried some heavy packs, but nothing remotely like the one that day. I also had a large billy full of rice to manage and, of course, my rifle. Darryl's was no easier. It usually takes around ninety minutes for that trip. But normal doesn't apply to a back-busting, leg-shaking grind, which was the way that walk turned out to be.

Three hours later we had almost reached journey's end when an animal emerged from the trees below us and began to feed on a steep carpet of green. I swung down my pack, flung up the rifle and downed the beast very smartly.

'Jeez,' cried Darryl, looking furtively about as if he expected a musterer to suddenly appear. 'You've gone and shot a sheep.'

'Well, damn me,' I said in wonder, 'so I have.'

'It was only about twenty yards away. Didn't you know it was a sheep?'

'Hell, no!' I replied, giving him my rifle and rice to carry and dragging the mutton down towards the hut. 'I figured it was a grey woolly deer.'

Sorry about that, Ngamatea.

The old dilapidated Manson hut is in a sheltered spot and though it belongs to the largest sheep station in the North Island — Ngamatea — we Kaweka hunters had the use of it.

Inside it's very spacious, the dirt floor has been trampled over the years to something like concrete, and although it's well ventilated the interior stank a little. However, after

The mighty red stag.

scrubbing down the big grimy possum-toilet table, and leaving the door wide open, the air cleared considerably.

Then in the evening, while Darryl collected wood I did a stroll for meat, and didn't have to go far.

It was quite pleasant that night. A huge fire lit the far, dark corners and we had several candles going. There was, at the Manson hut, a camp oven to end all camp ovens. It's about five times the size of the normal Forestry A-type and weighs a ton. Well, almost. I expect it's still there. We

When a red stag is well worked up, as this one was, it is possible, by convincing him that you also possess antlers, to bring him right up to you.

figured that the best way of making our food spin out was a stew, so first of all we cut up the back legs of the sheep into small pieces and also one of the two legs of venison that I'd brought back, and then added peas, rice, macaroni, barley, potatoes, salt, pepper, and a dash of Worcester sauce plus a little flour and some Marmite.

As it cooked I suddenly laughed out loud.

'All right,' asked Darryl, looking up from his book, 'what's the big joke?'

'I just remembered that salad you made at Makahu Saddle hut a couple of months back, mate.'

He took a deep puff on his Midway cigar, told me what to do with my laugh, and went back to reading.

So you'll have to forgive me here, Darryl, but it's far too good to leave out. Makahu Saddle is pretty much sika deer territory. Darryl and I had been hunting from the hut there for a couple of days and neither of us had scored. (Nothing new when up against sika.) A much-needed airdrop was due soon, but with no venison and not much else either, the evening meal did present a problem. However, as it was Darryl's turn to cook I let him do the worrying. Then dramatically he bounded off his bunk: 'I'm going to make us a salad.'

I merely nodded, but I did wonder. Greens are mighty scarce around Makahu Saddle way. But this didn't bother Darryl at all, and whistling cheerfully if not tunefully, he smartly set about making his concoction. Thirty minutes later it was ready and there on my tin plate was a heap of cold mixed vegetables straight from the can, a small mound of yesterday's cold spuds, and the lot was saturated with mayonnaise made with condensed milk. Salad *à la* Steele.

'What's it like?' he asked anxiously after I'd tried several mouthfuls.

'Not so bad,' I managed to say, as my teeth were practically stuck together by this mess, 'but how about some spaghetti instead?'

Meantime our stew was starting to simmer in the old Manson hut and the aroma was enough to make one drool. In this case, two.

It was fine and cool the following morning after a frosty night and, with two helpings of that solid but solid stew pushing hard against my shorts, I moved swiftly in on a bellowing stag. His peevish moans, angry grunts and lusty roars had me quite keyed up. But, as I came close, a hush fell over the wide bush valley. This was annoying, as the stag and several others had been performing well for the last half-hour. Perhaps they needed some encouragement, I thought, so cupping my hands together I roared: a pathetic, falsetto effort indeed, but it did the trick. A far beast answered and that prompted the one I was stalking to become vocal again. I crept forward slowly, and there he was, taking out his anger on a low bush with a small rack of white-tipped antlers. Suddenly he paused, his head came well back and his challenge rang out. Immediately three more from various distant parts joined in. I fired then at a range of less than thirty yards and it was an easy shot.

During the next few days the roar reached its peak. The majority of stags were, I found, teamed up with a single hind or, if they had been luckier, three or four. Others were on their own, perhaps their technique wasn't all that it should be — still, we can't all be lover-boys. Darryl and I ate much stew and hunted hard. A memorable incident from the roar on the Manson was where a steep, fernclad ridge dropped to a cascading creek and a stag was bellowing from deep within him. He was beneath me and out of sight owing to the very heavy, jungle-like undergrowth.

Joe Houghton glassing for red deer in his beloved Rimutaka Range.

When a red stag is well worked up, as this one was, it is possible, by convincing him that you also possess antlers, to bring him right up to you. For this you must have the wind in your favour, plenty of patience, and more than a little luck. This one was well worth a go, so to start with I gave a low moan; I have much more success with that than if I try to imitate a big fellow in full voice. And right away, no messing about, the stag replied with a roar which almost shook the beech trees. I tried another and so did he. A few slow minutes slipped by. I moaned again; no answer this time. Ten minutes or so passed. A distant beast was carrying on, but from the close one, nothing. I stood up slowly and immediately noticed a faint wind trailing downhill. Damn, I thought, he must have got wind of me.

I decided to have a look further down and, as I skirted a patch of high beech bush, I was suddenly face to face with a flabbergasted stag. I don't know which of us got the greater shock. He gave a startled sort of grunt and flung himself violently backwards, and at the same time I tripped over a hidden root and sprawled face-down in the fern. I came up

quickly, but he was already out of sight and only the acrid odour they carry at this time of year remained.

I yelled out then at the stag as he hadn't gone far and was making a hell of a racket, and to my amazement he stopped and replied with a blood-and-guts roar. He was quiet for a moment, then, as I remained perfectly still, I could hear this heavy body crashing back through the dense growth towards me. As he came lunging into view, steam rising from his body and ready to take on anything, I fired at his chest, which completely filled the scope. The range was less than five yards. I knelt down then, next to the fallen one and, as I calmed down inside, wouldn't have changed places with anyone.

After a week we left the Manson. The weather had been good and the hunting fine, but oh that stew, day in and day out.

Rocks-Ahead hut was the next port of call and it was great to be in a warm camp once more. The first thing I did, after unpacking and brewing up, was to make a batch of fried scones. They didn't last long either.

Good weather came with Good Friday, so I decided to hunt up on Back Ridge. Without a pack I made the ridge-top in ninety minutes and called in at the bivvy for afternoon coffee. As I sat on the sunlit step, a faint but distinct roar came from well along the ridge. Gulping the rest of my drink I set off smartly. Well, I had me a choice, as there were two stags performing — one each side of the ridge. The one on the slopes above the Ngaruroro sounded the most worked up, so I decided to try for him, and in no time at all I was back on the ridge with a tail. By now the other stag, on the Kiwi Creek side, was going better than before. Much better.

He'd set up camp some distance into the forest, in a

grass- and fern-carpeted basin that contained a large and very dirty waterhole. (Stags love to wallow during the roar.) My first view of him was of black-stained antlers flung back, and he was grunting away at a rapid rate. Close by I spotted his harem, a harem of one who fed quite unperturbed by it all. Still, I guess she'd heard it all before. Two more kills. It was well after dark when I neared Rocks-Ahead. So dark, that finding my way along the track as it wound between the trees and through the deep fern was a slow, tiresome business indeed. Then suddenly and from just off the track came the most unearthly noise, one which riveted me to the spot for the moment and, quite frankly, damn near scared the daylights out of me. It's just as well that I knew what it was, or I'd have been heading for the hut in a panic-stricken run, dark or not. Again the sika stag roared — a version that began on a low pitch and gradually worked up to the level of a banshee wailing its head off amid some Irish bog. Moving just off the track and with the rifle cocked, I peered hard in his direction. But he didn't roar again, nor did I catch even a shadowy glimpse; and he must have gone on tiptoes, for his departure was soundless.

Several days later Darryl had moved to Back Ridge hut and I was camped at the bivvy on Back Ridge and had turned in for the night. I was dreaming, but this dream seemed to consist solely of a roaring stag. I woke abruptly and discovered that it was no dream: close by, a stag was roaring continuously. A quick glance at my watch told me it was three thirty. I stepped outside — the clearing was brilliantly lit by a full moon. At that moment the stag was quiet, so I tried a roar, and a second or two later came a deep reply. Quickly I dressed and angled up towards the stag. I had hoped that he would be in the open, but he was a little way into the forest. Many stags were roaring well on that frosty night but, with the exception of this handy one, they were all well down towards Kiwi Creek. Perhaps thirty yards from the high black face of the forest I crouched beside a low bush. The stag roared again, and I decided to try and lure him out into the open. It wouldn't be easy.

I tried a deep grunt, then a lowish moan, and although the stag had not been vocal at that moment, I could almost sense a sudden, thoughtful silence on his part. Now what's this? he possibly thought. Again I moaned. Then from the direction of the stag I could plainly hear a violent cracking of branches, quiet for a moment, and then a lusty bellow. Another from me … an answer … my turn … and then he was grunting and smashing his way towards me. And, as the black outline that was the stag left the trees at a brisk walk, I groped for him in the scope like a sightless man. Unable to pick him up I lowered the weapon and immediately cried out, no doubt in fright, as he was almost upon me. At the sound of my voice he halted, at once unsure. This time, with the forest no longer a direct backdrop, I found his neck silhouetted clearly. The shot rang out and the stag thumped down. He was, I later measured, just three yards away. I looked at my watch then — it was just 3.44 a.m. A very early morning shot.

That was my first roar, and that first time is just that bit more significant than the rest. The one, I feel, that seems to stay a whole lot sharper in your memory.

But each roar is exciting. Each one gives the hunter thrilling moments that he can look back upon, when the hills have become just too steep for ageing legs, and that driving urge to hunt is no more.

Hunter by Profession — 1973

In Bush Country

The trophy-sized antlers of a sika stag in plain sight at very close range.
The ear of a hind can be seen at the left side of the photograph.

Whichever way you looked at it I really couldn't have picked a worse time to take on meat shooting than the winter of 1970. Apart from the fact that deer are mostly bushbound during the winter months, it always seemed to be raining and the rivers were running high. I was stopped quite frequently from going up anywhere but the Hikurangi Stream. Then occasionally it snowed heavily and that, I found, was just as loathsome as I remembered it for hunting. Apart from the infrequent fine days it was bitterly cold with a southerly gusting up the riverbeds and whipping through the trees. At such times the forest moaned like a thing alive. As I've said, I could have picked a better time. After nearly two months of walking waist-deep up freezing rivers in the first light, and then pushing on through the lower, soaking forest to where I'd really begin stalking, I couldn't wait for the warmer months to arrive. But as Lyn sympathetically said when I reached home one bleak evening with hands so useless I couldn't undo my bootlaces: 'Well, luv, you wanted to be a hunter again.'

A sound point.

Coming home after such days to a hot drink, a long, luxuriant soak in the bath, and dinner before a blazing log fire seemed to make it all worthwhile.

Bush shooting became extremely tiresome, but it was never less than a challenge. Indeed, of all the various kinds of terrain that a hunter encounters in New Zealand, that which is classed as bush country must surely be the ultimate test in hunting ability.

It's true that most hunters can, and frequently do during the spring and summer months, shoot any amount of game on the river-flats and open tussock tops. But those who can score consistently where the cover is thick are definitely in the minority. It takes time before one becomes proficient in the forest. There are no short cuts that I know of.

Perhaps the best way to lead into this chapter on bush shooting would be like this: The hissing Coleman lamp, ringed by persistent droning insects and smelling dreadfully of kerosene, lit up the picturesque interior of the small hut that long-ago evening when I was hunting for the Forest Service. Fresh venison backsteaks, sliced extra thin and beaten hard with a stick before cooking, sizzled next to thickly sliced onions and chipped potatoes in the A-type camp oven. After a hard but good day on the hill it was just fine to feel clean warm clothing on one's body, dry socks instead of wet; to listen to the National Transistor 10 blaring out hit parade music.

As I prepared dinner my much younger companion sat dejectedly on the edge of his bunk. It was a position he'd immediately taken up on coming into the hut; without removing his now steaming clothing or waterlogged boots. That, I'd better add, was a full hour back — long enough to have him shivering, even if it was snug and cosy inside the hut. His day's effort had been a dismal affair. He hadn't even spotted a deer. I knew how he felt; what hunter doesn't? But the country we had stalked offered, in my opinion, top-notch bush shooting, with his area for the day perhaps shading mine a little. It was this and nothing else that was really getting to my mate; he simply couldn't do any good in this, or any other, bush country. It wasn't for the lack of trying, either. In fact, he'd spent a full eight hours on the hill that day.

As the long winter evening dragged on, his fuzz-clad jaw dropped lower and lower until it finally rested solidly on his chest. In a voice full of despair he told me that he was giving the game away; that his professional hunting days were over. That, to me, seemed like such a waste. He'd proved that he could handle his rifle on target and, better still, that he could do the same on game. It wasn't only that, though, because he was normally a happy, carefree type — a clean one too, and one who did his share and perhaps a little more around camp. Besides, he had been a pro-shooter for only six months which, I consider, is hardly time enough to know how a bloke's going to turn out.

To excel at hunting takes years, not months, unless, of course, one is the type it all comes to so naturally that there is no real effort required to become what's known in the game as a 'gun' hunter. But such men, I've found, are as common as our moose.

To try and shake him out of his depressed mood I told him of some of the things which had happened to me since I'd taken up hunting as a living. Things like mistaking a spot-lighted cattle beast for a sambar deer; and the time I shot a small bush simply because, by a remarkable trick of the sun, it appeared exactly like a deer. This, I hate to admit, actually happened with a scope-sighted rifle. (Still, I'm in good company when it comes to doing stupid things with a rifle; for I have yet to meet a hunter who, if sufficiently pressed, doesn't own up to at least one 'classic' mistake.)

Much to my surprise it did the trick and soon he was back to normal. He even began to ask me questions on what I'd learnt over the years about bush hunting, which surprised me even further. This was something he could have done before but, in his case at least, I didn't think he wanted to admit he was lacking in any way whatsoever when it came to hunting. I could — and can — understand this kind of attitude. With perhaps a few exceptions, we all fall into this same category during our early days.

Because he was genuinely interested in what I had to say and not just sitting there with a polite, slightly bored expression and hearing absolutely nothing, I covered such things as where to seek animals in the bush; when to and how to best go about it. I also pointed out that real know-how in the forest was something which he'd only pick up with personal experience; and that no book or no one, however helpful and instructive, could really teach him about that. I also mentioned that many pro-shooters, the ones who flogged the open country to death, had long since given up the thought of ever making real bush hunters.

When he asked why, I really had to think deeply. Perhaps, I finally said, it's not in all of us to excel at this kind of hunting; that there must be some basic leaning towards it to begin with. I also added, and quickly too, that this was only my theory.

With the help of numerous brews I must have yarned away for a couple of hours. It was a fine effort for someone who's been called taciturn at times. That young bloke turned out to be a fine bush hunter in time, probably one of the best around from what I've heard since. Naturally I don't kid myself that any real credit belongs to me. But I can feel that what I said could possibly have encouraged him to stay with it. I really like to think that.

In the hills I have often discussed bush shooting methods with others. Their views were often rewarding, sometimes hilarious, occasionally surprising; and now and then ridiculous.

As the most likely animal a hunter will encounter is the red deer, this is the one I'll select as the quarry. I'll kick off with the quality of patience, because of all the assets that a hunter should have, I can't think of a better. If a man learns anything at all from hunting, then he should learn patience. While every young hunter is just rarin' to go, or should be, he simply cannot be expected to do well for a start.

At this stage imagine that a large tract of forested country lies invitingly before us. A place in fact which is new to us but one which we intend to hunt frequently in the future if it lives up to our expectations. In this stretch of unbroken wilderness, as in all others, there will be hot spots for game and those which are otherwise. Those places that are cold and damp, because they miss out on much of the sun, are shunned by all wild animals. I don't think domestic ones would think too much of them either. The deer will venture there but only, you'll find, to pass quickly through to or from feeding grounds. So you too should travel swiftly past these dark and cheerless spots.

In bush country deer favour those slopes which receive more sunshine than others. The reason is simple for, quite apart from it being infinitely more pleasant there, the growth is sure to be more lush, more advanced. And those places which are sheltered from the prevailing wind would, I think, be the real pick of where to look.

Over the years I've found that sheltered and sunny spots attract all creatures — deer and goats, pigs and 'roos love nothing better. From what I've learnt, and keeping in mind the sun and wind also, the real year-round pick is fairly high, say where the forest begins to peter out and blends into the sub-alpine vegetation and snowgrass. Then I have also found the heads of creeks, which are frequently basin-like in shape, to be a fine choice too. Now that you've located a very likely looking area — and this will be rather obvious by the sign, both recent and old, scattered liberally about — the smart move is to hunt there when it's to your advantage. To yours, not the deer's.

A popular notion concerning bush stalking is that it really doesn't matter what the time of day is. This is an opinion which shows up the novice or someone who hasn't learnt anything. Take the middle of the day when, speaking generally as one always must about wild game, deer are not in the least bit interested in anything but resting. This seems to last from nine o'clock in the morning until three in the afternoon, although a real hot day will have them lying down considerably longer.

The places they seek to rest up are normally where the cover is ample and good. Often, and more so when it's windy, they may prefer to stay in the fern. And there doesn't seem to be a shortage of that anywhere. They could perhaps select a spot which enables them to see a great deal. A ridge is often selected for this purpose. They usually face downhill into the wind which has a marked tendency to drift up in hilly country. But even while the deer rests, that moist shiny black nose is active. It is in fact just as sensitive and just as questing as ever. Those large, hairy, funnel-shaped ears are constantly flickering about. But the bedded deer is still. Perfectly so. It blends in with its background, even, it seems, when it is wearing its bright summer coat. It's often out of sight when a man is only a few yards away. This is especially so in the fern.

What I'm really trying to say is this: the odds all favour the deer. So this, then, is the animal you'll most likely encounter during the hours I've mentioned. While I have known many hunters to do really well at this time of day, it is nevertheless difficult in comparison with before and after the resting time.

I much prefer to bush hunt in the late afternoon and, if possible, right up to dark. That last hour of light in good bush-hunting country is really something. The main reason for my preference is that you can be right on the spot when it counts, whereas with the morning it's usually getting late by the time you get where you want to. Another thing: there won't be any deer resting then. They're either eating up large on their way smartly to a popular bush restaurant. And these deer, either scoffing or on the move, are a completely different proposition from what they were a few hours before.

Grassy clearings are tops with deer too; more so in the spring and particularly when they're covered with a profusion of nettles and hookgrass, as is common in the Urewera country. But a man will come to know it all in time, to go through the motions instinctively. It's then, only then, that he will really come into his own.

The bush shooter will quickly learn that the wind is his arch-enemy. I'd much rather spend thirty minutes with it favouring me than any amount of time the other way. I can't remember ever surprising a deer in the bush with the wind directly behind me. Plenty of smoking tracks, though. Bush hunting really depends on the type of country it is, deer sign, and the wind. A man must often hunt at the discretion of the wind.

On really cold and windy days you're wasting your time looking anywhere that's not well sheltered. That's why the tops are right out in such conditions. Deer have no liking for the wind. Red deer have an absolutely fantastic sense of smell, but also, in my opinion, indifferent eyesight and hearing that, while not razor-sharp, is still extra-keen. If we have the wind to our advantage, then it's obvious we won't be winded. We might, however, be spotted or heard. There is much less chance of this if we wear gear which blends well with the general backdrop, and is of a type which

The vast Urewera country and adjacent wilderness where bush hunting is very much the order of the day.

makes little noise whenever it catches anything. Nylon and Japara parkas, leather, and all oiled jackets are right out, since they make a terrific scraping noise when brushing against undergrowth and scrub which not only scares game but also goes right through the wearer.

I like to have a woollen Swanndri for bush hunting in the winter, in either a shade of grey or drab olive green: a heavy pure wool shirt for the autumn and cooler days of spring and, for the hot months, an ex-army shirt, usually jungle green. But one of course often needs warm gear during the summer. The high country has always had the annoying habit of mixing the seasons up.

Footwear is of prime importance if you intend moving with the least noise possible. Leather boots with heavy commando-type soles are comparatively quiet, the dead opposite to nailed boots, which are bloody useless in the timber. Many North Island deer cullers have preferred ankle-length rubber boots, which I also used while hunting in Kaingaroa forest. They were just fine on the flat Kaingaroa plains but I've never felt really safe with them in mountainous terrain. Still, a lot of hunters wouldn't wear anything else. That's okay with me as long as they stick to leather boots in the summer. Have you ever been with a mate when, at the end of a long hot day, he's finally taken his gumboots off?

Really tops in my book, for the most silent stalking of all, are basketball boots; and being ankle-high they allow one to use puttees. Here again the country must be relatively easy for they offer little if any real protection for your feet. And where are you if they pack up back of beyond? Perhaps

Marlin .30-30 carbine.

I've placed too much emphasis on moving silently; but I happen to derive an enormous kick from moving right up to unsuspecting deer. It's a far better way than having one see you first or hearing that always frustrating sound of one crashing away unseen. It's hunting in the fullest meaning of the word.

When bush hunting it pays to look more than move — sometimes to crouch down if it will give you a better view. I usually travel at a steady sort of pace in the forest; only slowing down on reaching a spot which, because I know it's so right, screams out 'deer' to me. Then I put everything I have into it. At this stage I'd better add that there are other men who, regardless, keep to their same swift gait. They believe that by covering a great deal more country they'll see more animals. And they're right too. They rely on their ability to sneak up on a spooked deer; on their snap-shooting prowess as one runs for it. Both are generally considerable. Keith Lane and, if I remember rightly, Peter Cook, were of this school — and, as anyone who knew either as cullers will tell you, they were second to none in the art of collecting tails whenever and wherever they stalked.

But a man has to be himself, to hunt his own way. I cannot race through a likely-looking spot, I must always move quietly. That's the way most of us are as well. Even when you're placing your feet with the utmost care, when you're trying your hardest not to make the slightest noise, and even when you're really looking, a deer will often be aware of you first. They may not have winded, heard or spotted you. But something will have told them — that certain something which seems to be present in all wild creatures. It's then that you have to shoot quickly, and quite frequently there isn't much of a target.

I couldn't count the number of times I've just seen a large inquisitive head staring at me, or when all I had to go with it was a neck. In time you'll handle this kind of shooting with ease — if you get enough practice. It isn't easy for the non-professional to attain it for he simply doesn't do enough hunting to get beyond that woeful buck-fever stage.

Generally, a deer will hightail it on seeing or hearing you. It will certainly do so if it has caught your scent and knows exactly where you are. Judging by their behaviour on that count, the man smell must be very distressing indeed to deer. A deer will normally be out of sight within seconds of taking off, our bush country being what it is, but it won't go far before stopping. This is a habit of deer — red deer, I mean — that you can count on. For instance: a hind, if somehow separated from her young, certainly will not travel far before coming to a halt. She'll begin barking then, if she hasn't already done so. This is something which an unsure deer will also do.

If a deer does start barking continually at me, then I'm reasonably certain that's it's not quite sure what I am. It may have heard my boot catch a hidden root; perhaps some of my equipment made a metallic noise. Although it winded me good and proper, it may stay close simply because it's curious. That's quite likely if you happen to come across a sika … In circumstances such as this you must move up with all the caution you can possibly muster: eyes searching, rifle up and ready for a snapshot. Because there is one thing you can be sure of: that deer will be watching its back trail.

A deer that barks will often move a short distance between each vocal effort at a rapid walk-trot. This makes it almost impossible to catch up with if the undergrowth is really thick. Besides, in that type of country it's almost sure to hear you move up. It's very different in more open bush. The odds there I'd say would be roughly 50–50 for getting close enough for a shot.

While on the subject of barking deer I can well remember hearing a hind (it's usually the female) barking like a frantic sheep dog in fairly clear bush in the Manson country, at the back of Ngamatea station. She couldn't possibly have heard me; I was too far away for the most acute pair of ears. She may have momentarily caught my scent, even if the wind did seem to blow from her to me. But I don't know really. What I do know is that she was barking furiously and trotting around a smallish clearing in a tight circle when I spotted her.

One does see some strange animal behaviour at times. One late morning on the Tukituki block on the eastern side of the Ruahine Range I was glassing a flattish ridge from high above it when a spiker emerged out of the high bush edge and ran, flat out, from one end to the other, a distance of at least three hundred yards. Then, with hardly time to catch its breath, it raced all the way back. Coming to a sudden halt it propped, spun around, tossed its head like a frisky horse and then began bucking. I was amazed, never having seen such goings-on from a deer before. Vastly amused too. His bucking over — and it would have done credit to an untamed bronco — he galloped to the far end of the ridge again before calling it a day and vanishing into the trees. I could only put it down to high spirits; since they're quite common in the young. It turned out that the spiker was the only deer I saw that morning, but in no way did I consider my early rise a waste of time.

It's worth listening a great deal when you are in the bush for, quite contrary to many beliefs, no deer moves without some kind of noise, however minute. We're usually making far too much racket ourselves to take advantage of it.

One of the few times I can recall still hunting — a method that's popular in the eastern states of North America and where a hunter picks out a spot and waits for a deer to show up — occurred in the twin-lakes scrublands below and east of the Kaweka Range. I was looking over a grassy clearing that I'd visited on several recent evenings, a clearing on which the growth was thick that spring. The droppings of stags were littered everywhere and it seemed as if they'd been using it for weeks. So this evening I was going to sit and wait and see what, if anything, eventuated. Really pleasant it was, just waiting. And besides, I'd had more than enough of poking my way about the heavy manuka. There was just enough breeze to cause the clearing's only occupant — a splendid cabbage tree — to rustle slightly. The westering sun was dipping out of sight beyond the huge, dark bulk of the main Kaweka Range, and friendly birds flitted curiously about me.

It was rapidly approaching dark and I was on the point of giving it away when heavy bodies came crashing through the scrub towards the open. I wasn't surprised when two stags burst into view. You would have thought that, being of the wild, they'd have approached with great stealth, perhaps stuck a tentative head out of the scrub first. But not those two. They hit that feeding ground at a smart trot and promptly attacked the green fodder. Caution didn't come into it.

On other occasions, usually when I've been having a spell, I've heard deer feeding. Red stags and spikers, I soon discovered in the Urewera, could be very noisy when reaching high to browse on low-hanging foliage. So look a lot. Listen a lot.

The smell of a deer can often help you to locate one in close country. It's very noticeable that a non-smoker fares far better here. Red stags are really high during their rut — a powerful, pungent odour and no mistake. It can result in a

Wary indeed is this young sika stag. From this angle, the V-shaped tops of his antlers cannot be seen; however, the white chin patch, typical of the breed, is clearly visible.

hunter finding his stag by first smelling him. Some red hinds have their more smelly moments too, caused when, from a resting position, they urinate on themselves.

If you suddenly get a strong smell of a deer, then it can mean only two things: it's close or it's just been there. Either way you'd better freeze; the deer might be only yards away.

Or it might not. When I was bush-bashing near Te Pukeohikarua hut (how I love to roll my tongue around that) in the Kawekas, the sharp scent of a deer brought me to a full stop. The forest was practically bare of undergrowth for a distance of about one hundred yards. The smell didn't fade slowly away as it so often does. I hadn't moved, but I had looked everywhere with no result. The wind was racing through the trees, causing dead leaves to swirl about. Moving into it I slowly covered a few yards, then paused again. The smell was still there. Still powerful too. I had another prolonged look. Nothing. Moved on some more and, as I did, the smell gradually became more intense. It led me out of the open through a belt of fern to the edge of some high undergrowth. It was now so strong that I'm sure a chain smoker with a severe bout of hay fever could have smelt it.

A red hind — this was sika territory too — rocketed up when I sneaked into her hideout and as luck would have it, escaped. I'd had a reasonable day: four according to my diary, so it didn't bother me unduly. It wouldn't have made much difference if I hadn't scored either. You learn to take those days when you dip out with a shrug. Or should. I was curious to know how far I'd actually winded her from, so I paced it out. It came to one hundred and eighty long steps. That was an exception. Those which I've winded first have usually been within thirty or fifty yards of me.

Very recently, as a meat shooter, I returned to a once favoured bush-hunting haunt of mine. It had known continual shooting pressure since I'd last been there from both professional and private shooters. Yet in no way whatsoever had it changed. The deer still frequented the same localities. Because of this I was soon able to locate a couple. But this, once you are really familiar with an area, is bush hunting.

As always I derived far more satisfaction out of making a kill in this kind of terrain than in any other, because this is when you must think like a deer and, to be consistently successful, out-think them.

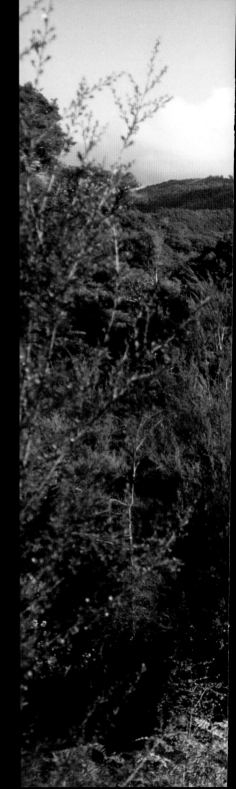

by Profession — 1973

Sika

One of New Zealand's outstanding deer is, without a doubt, the sika. This is so much so that most hunting trips after them turn out to be ones to remember. Even though I devoted a chapter to sika in my first book I feel that, where they are concerned, I still have plenty to say. And since they're comparatively unwritten about in book form I really can't resist having another go.

I'll start this way: I'd heard a great deal about sika before reaching the Kawekas. Some of the Kaingaroa hunters (where I was hunting until then) had been up against them and the thrilling stories they told would've made any hunter keen to match his ability against sika.

It wasn't until September 1962 that I found myself closing a hut door and setting off for my first hunt in real sika territory. The hut was the Lawrence — a log-framed affair built some ten years previously by Morrie and Carol Robson: it was a real cosy camp with, I thought, a great deal of character.

There were three others there then: Jim Stegmann, Hank Christensen, and Geoff Beale. I've never camped with a better trio. Jim had taken off for one of his favourite spots, Happy Valley; Hank went up the Donald River; Geoff along the track which leads to Lotkow hut. We'd only arrived at the hut that day and headman Jim's last words were: 'Bring back as much meat as you can, boys.'

The evening was cool after a windy but fine sort of day as I headed down the Tutaekuri River which weaved between fairly steep, heavily forested hills. Being shallow and warm it was quite pleasant to travel, too.

It's a wonderful feeling to be hunting where you might strike a different game animal: you're all tense, excited and just bursting to spot one. My idea was to travel a good

distance downstream and then cut up into the bush. 'That's where they'll be, Phil,' Geoff had said.

So I was a long way from being prepared for a nearby whistle — way, way up in the falsetto range. Somewhat distorted by the slight noise of the wind and the deeper racket of the river it brought me to an abrupt, excited halt in the middle of the third crossing. I knew what it belonged to all right.

I quickly glanced over a narrow, grassy slip which angled down to the river bottom. Not a thing. Then along the rocky river surrounds. Again a blank. Where the hell is it, I wondered, for that whistle had seemed so very close. Then again, and while I still wondered, that curious noise rang out again. Yet again it was hard to pinpoint. Yet again my eyes searched hard. Yet again — nothing!

Probably it's a little inside the bush edge, I decided. Then I saw it and it wasn't on that grassy slip, or close to the river; and it wasn't in the trees either, but actually knee-deep in the Tutaekuri!

I was using a Parker Hale .303 then. (One that Geoff Beale had sold to me for a fiver and one which eventually went back to him for the same price. Frankly, we should both have been paid for using the thing.) Anyway, I flung that rusty, ill-fitting rifle to my shoulder, groping for the rump-on sika in the aperture sight. As I did that the sika bolted — directly away. And suddenly there was another smaller one crowding its racing heels. Now where, I thought in an exasperated fashion, had that one come from?

Just in case you've never lined up on a fleeing sika I'd better put you right in the picture. Their run is a rapid, jerky and bobbing one which makes it extremely difficult to get a good bead. And with that pathetic sight I couldn't. So I held

Arguably the North Island's top game animal — a sika stag and hind during the roar.

fire, despite a strong urge to chance a shot. I just hoped that, like red deer, they'd stop for a brief look back. The leading one, which I thought was a hind, had now left the river and was leaping up a crumbling bank with small-fry right behind it. And right on the top of the bank, with the trees only a long jump away, they stopped and looked back to where the danger lay.

I knew it was, to use a cliche, a case of right now or never and, like a cool old hand, yanked back hard on the stiff trigger. A 'thunk' came back to me a second or two before the hind's legs abruptly folded beneath her. Down, with a gathering momentum, she rolled back to the water's edge. I'd instantly set about ejecting the spent cartridge but, by the time I'd crashed another round home the younger sika was gone. The hind was still when I reached her and, looking down, I thought that I had never seen a more pretty and gracefully built animal.

Whenever I begin to think about sika mental flashbacks begin to crowd my mind, so quickly at times that I have to pause and sort them out. I can recall Geoff Beale coming into Makahu Saddle hut with a sad, withdrawn look about him. This wasn't easy-going, good-natured Geoff at all. So I asked him what was wrong. I learnt that he'd come across a deer in the last lingering moments of daylight, a deer he didn't miss. But to Geoff's great dismay it turned out to be a sika stag in the velvet. That's nothing new for a culler — it's on all the time. The one that Geoff had shot, however, was, in his words, a real beaut. It had, said Geoff sadly, eight

Teal Bay hut. When you have been wet all day and your hands are blue with cold, a hut like this is a sweet sight indeed.

well-developed points of a fine length and spread and would surely have measured out as a real trophy. And that's what had upset Geoff: it was such a rotten waste.

'You know, Phil?' said Geoff. 'I'd never have shot him if I'd known just how good his antlers really were.'

There are very few professional hunters who would have been as upset as Geoff. But then Geoff Beale was a most unusual professional hunter.

Then I can remember sinking my teeth into my first sika steak a few days after scoring that sika hind down the Tutaekuri. We'd all brought meat back that evening at the Lawrence, all two hind legs in fact.

We'd eaten red deer venison for a start, letting the sika meat mature a little first. Yes, I remember sinking my teeth into that first feed of sika all right and thinking, how fantastic it was in direct comparison to the dry, frequently tasteless venison of our common deer, the red.

It also requires no effort to visualise my hunting cobber on the Mangaohane block, Dick Hart, striding through wet, waist-deep tussock towards me with a seven-point set of sika antlers which he'd collected near Makerikeri hut strapped on to his bulging pack. Then, later, the look of pride as he told me of it.

Then there are the sika themselves: lightning-fast, ultra-smart, highly vocal, curious to a fault, exceedingly handsome in appearance.

At one stage there was a considerable amount of controversy over whether or not sika and red deer crossed.

At that time there were as many said they did as didn't. Morrie Robson, who'd learnt much about both red and sika, was convinced that they did. I didn't believe him. That is until I was stalking high in Kiwi Creek, a small, closed-in creek which joins the Ngaruroro River near Kiwi Mouth hut.

Around four o'clock I was wishing that I'd hunted elsewhere for the undergrowth was much too thick for quiet hunting. The closest I'd come to a deer had just been the smell of one. Then it happened. A stag came up from his resting spot just before me in one flowing movement. He kept going, too, which meant he was out of sight after a few huge bounds. I moved after him and, as I'd picked, he hadn't gone far.

This stag turned out to be some animal. For a start his head was large, unmistakeably red, except for the distinct bat-shaped ears which are typical of sika. The antlers — in the velvet — were a deep golden orange and well covered with black blotches, yet again sika. The size, however, was that of a red deer and, to top it off, its tail was that of a red deer.

At that very moment, miles away to the north, a Forest Service research team was carrying out an extensive survey on the sika deer. How I'd have loved to have staggered into one of their camps with this stag on my back. But as it most likely weighed a good three hundred pounds on the hoof …

I agreed with Morrie after that.

To wrap up this chapter, and to give you an idea what hunting sika can be like, I'll go back to a hot day in Kaweka country. Besides the heat it was blowing hard, as it normally is on the Kaweka tops. Heading north the range made a sweeping curve, so that below, on the eastern side, it resembled a vast amphitheatre. The sides here fell sharply away to a good-sized basin. Down there, reflecting the fine day, was a tarn and, close to it, a small stand of trees, while below the lip of the basin heavy bush slopes swept up from flattish scrublands. Down there seemed a far better proposition than where I was.

All the same I hesitated. I was hunting from Back Ridge hut and, if I went down there, it meant that I'd have to climb all the long hard way back. I thought about my mate Geoff Beale, and how we'd split the country within hunting radius from Back Ridge for our stay there: Geoff the bush, which meant Kiwi Creek, and I the open tops, which I'd wanted. Since it had been tremendously windy every day, and since deer don't dig that, Geoff, being one hell of a fine bush hunter, had scored every time he went out. His mate, on the other hand, was starting to forget what they looked like. A sad state of affairs and no mistake.

In typical Beale fashion, Geoff offered to change around now that the conditions definitely favoured the bush. But I wasn't having any of that. I'd wanted the open country. I'd got the open country. I was stuck with it! I guess that's one of the reasons why I've always preferred to camp on my own — you can hunt just where you wish. And when. So I reckon that's why I didn't hesitate too long about going well over on the eastern side of the range. It was time something else was hanging from my belt besides a knife-sheath and first-aid kit …

I travelled to the basin quickly, zigzagging down a long, narrow shingle slide. For a start I looked over the basin, then around the sun-dried mud surrounds of the tarn. The waterhole didn't look blue down here — just brown and scum-covered. I'd have needed to be rather desperate for a drink to have tried that. Then I moved into the clump of well-spaced trees: all mountain beech. There wasn't a sign of deer there, recent or otherwise. That gave it something in common with the rest of the basin.

Another slip beginning below the lip of the basin looked like a fast way to the forest. And so it proved to be. As I cut into the trees, a sika squealed. And it didn't sound too far away either. I waited for the deer to become vocal again, knowing that it would. When the sika obliged a few moments later it seemed to have come from above, back above the slip, in fact. Moving back to the bush edge I peered up, spotting a big-eared head gazing warily down. I wondered just how she'd got there; it was only a few minutes at the most since I'd been in that very same spot. Strange. The sika — a hind — was at an awkward angle to me. To make it much worse she only displayed her head and neck. I was considering a shot when the decision was made up for me. The sika hind had gone. It took no time at all to reach the spot where the hind had looked down from the basin, for it's marvellous just how inspired one can become at such a moment.

There wasn't a sign of her and, rubbing my whiskered jaw, I wondered where she'd gone. That is until she whistled once again. Then I knew. She'd set up a temporary camp in the stand of trees. These mountain beech, on the far side of the tarn from me, were lower than my present spot. Much lower. It meant that if I moved, and if the hind should run out of the far side, then I'd not see her.

Much better, I thought, to stay put, to play the waiting

game. While I reached this decision the sika had whistled, had squealed, had run up and down the scale with a series of grunts. It was quite a performance and I was suitably impressed.

A short time passed; still she hadn't moved. At short intervals, however, she'd carry on in great style. Hoping to alarm her enough to scare her out I began to yell and whistle, but she plainly wasn't having any of that. In the trees suited her. And that was that! Action was called for. So I aimed into the trees and let one go. Even before the booming sound of the .303 had reverberated away, a spotted-coated streak burst out into the open. The far side of the trees, of course.

It wasn't a long shot, around one hundred yards I judged. And I was sitting down, too, which always helps. But I'm not a good shot on moving game — never have been. So I led her a good way and the round, landing a yard or two directly before her, did the trick. She came to a quick halt. By now the sika hind was all of two hundred yards away. But I was breathing easy and sitting as I've said. So there was no excuse really for the shot which took her in the stomach. It slowed her down to a leaden walk. I tried again holding a fraction before her moving chest. Over she went and rolled out of sight into a small hollow. Dead, too, when I got there.

Her coat, although still well spotted, was just starting to change and small tufts of it came away as I handled her. A pity, for I was on the lookout for a good summer sika skin for a friend. He wouldn't be getting it now. As I tailed the hind a squeal, loud and very close, had me twisting about and staring at two more sika. They were on the rim of the hollow, less than five yards from me and brilliantly outlined against the blue sky. (I later thought that the vocalising of the hind could have attracted them.) Again one of them squealed as they spun around and leapt out of sight. I sprang for my rifle, nearly tripping in my excitement.

Such was the speed of the sika that they'd already made the bush edge by the time I was in a position to shoot. While thinking whether or not it was worth following them up a whistle, seeming to come from just inside the forest, made my mind up for me. The forest, I quickly found, was real machete country, the kind of bush where the odds aren't with the hunter. It seemed they'd moved a little further into this jungle, that is to judge from the latest squeal. I thought they'd stay close for a time and, trying my utmost not to make the slightest noise, knowing that two pairs of sensitive ears were tuned in for anything out of the ordinary, I crept on.

Then I saw one. In fact, I'm sure we saw each other together. That's often the way.

At a moment like this it's hard to know what to do. Should you raise your rifle up slow and easy or as quickly as possible? Either one, at times, can be the wrong move. But that time I settled for a slow flowing uplift, nothing jerky. And the sika didn't move a muscle. That is until the rifle reached my shoulder, then it wasn't there any more. Gone. Just like that. And a wild crashing noise to my right was most likely the other one. I was to catch one more glimpse of one of them before they decided they'd had their fun, before I might just get lucky.

But that's sika hunting, really. And it's such behaviour which makes them second to none in the deer family.

Wild Goats: the
Big-Horn Breed

lower part of the North Island, like the
here, are of obvious Angora ancestry.

In the Otago Province, where this shot was taken, feral goats have been established since the 1860s and almost certainly stem from stock abandoned by gold diggers.

It's always amazed me the way many hunters tend to dismiss wild goats with a scornful shake of their heads. This is something which applies to local hunters more than any. Those from overseas are quite happy to fork out money for the privilege of hunting them. To them the wild goat is a trophy animal, worthy to be shoulder-mounted if the horns are close to, or better than, thirty inches. You often hear of goats being run in with a mob of sheep — or even deliberately mustered and then sold at low prices. Many hunters have their favourite yarn about when they shot up a mob.

'Stupid bloody lot!' they'll say later to their mates. 'Why, they just stood around while I shot them one by one.'

Well, this type of thing is indeed common when and where goats are semi-tame; those found over much of the Waihau area, and indeed Hawke's Bay, are farmland goats that anyone could clean up without half trying.

This chapter is about a different kind of animal: wild goats that know all about man by sight, smell, and the ugly crack of a high-powered rifle which invariably goes with him …

Sudden hail slashed against my face with a steady, driving insistence, and it wasn't doing my bare legs and face any good. A howling gale raced through the narrow, steep-walled gully I was hunting. Conditions could have been better.

As it was still fairly early in the day I decided to hole up somewhere until the weather cleared somewhat. In no time at all I spotted a large recess below an overhanging cliff-face. It was bone-dry here and right out of the wind. Against that, however, was a mighty powerful stink indeed: wild sheep. They were the scattered remnants of flocks of Merinos living on what was once cleared ground which had reverted to unbroken scrub. Still, the smell was far better than the hail and icy wind which had left my hands and face without any feeling whatsoever.

I suppose a man shouldn't have been hunting at all, for only a real mug would have left a warm hut and set forth into grim August conditions the way I had.

Along with three other government guns I had spent four days of just sitting and waiting for the lousy weather to pick up. Then on the fifth morning it did. By that, I mean the wind dropped to about thirty miles an hour and the solid grey wall of rain changed into a steady downpour.

Now, sitting on my haunches in a smelly cavern which was more of a scooped-out hollow, I couldn't help wishing I was sitting before the fire in Ruahine hut once more. Keith Lane, Barry Hunt and Leo Smith had the right idea all right: playing endless games of five hundred, listening to the transistor radio, and eating up large on camp-oven bread which has a habit of making a man a bit on the windy side.

But you get sick of the same old hairy faces and the same old conversation. So out I had gone. A walk down a long open ridge called The Seconds; the thrilling sight of the Ngaruroro way above normal level, thick with yellowish mud and scattered debris as it pounded along to the plains of Hawke's Bay. And now enjoying myself hugely in a stinking shelter.

Suddenly, high on the opposite cliff-face, a small greyish patch caught my eye. As this sheer wall of outward sloping rock was a shade of grey, too, I'd most likely not have spotted it if it hadn't moved a fraction.

Quickly checking through my scope I saw it was a wild goat. It, too, was well out of the weather, cramped up at the rear end of a shallow cave which was even more of a scooped-out hollow than where I was.

On account of the driving rain it wasn't much of a picture I had through the scope lens and it was also rather dark where the goat was. But I had the answer along with me: my 8x30s. Now the goat showed up good and clear. And so did the horns he carried. Why, I excitedly estimated, they must span at least thirty inches, maybe a bit more.

It wouldn't be easy to get him. Not that the range was great; the trouble was that the goat (providing I hit it) might fall on to rocky ground directly below. That was a drop, a straight one, of at least eighty feet which I knew would smash his horns completely. There had to be another way …

The goat was around 150 yards away and, to make it even more awkward, was revealing only the topmost parts of himself. Then it hit me! Why not try and scare him out into the open and let him move off the sheer cliff-face before shooting? On either side of the goat's possie were long and grassy guts. Once he was on either of these, even if he did roll a little way, it was unlikely he'd knock his horns about. Providing I hit him!

While I was reaching this decision, the hail and wind had abruptly packed it in. Now to get the billy off his backside and on the move.

Cupping my hands together I gave a loud yell — and then another because the first one caused no reaction at all. Perhaps the goat figured it made more sense to stay right where he was.

Obviously something of a more positive nature was called for: like a shot fairly close to him.

I raised the 7 mm rifle, sent a shot away, and that did the trick. Poised on the extreme rim of his resting place the billy goat, with his long grey-black mane ruffled slightly by the updraught and his wide and heavy horns spreading out above a blocky and deep-chested body, was indeed an impressive sight. An animal that had a look of real wilderness country upon him.

For a little while longer he stayed put — still, watchful, testing the wind. Then he angled along what must have been a minute track; a road for goats and sheep only. And in his ability to negotiate it he demonstrated the marvellous agility of his breed. It was really something to watch.

As he slowly came off the cliff-face and on to the green gut to my right I was following him through the scope, breathing real easy, the bolt closing all the way on 150 grains of soft-point Norma slug. Deadly this, for all medium game.

Then the BSA crashed out once more and the goat was lurching around like a drunken man for a full minute at least before suddenly rolling a short distance and piling up behind a deadfall.

It didn't take me long to reach him. Once I was there the length and thickness of horn delighted me. Suddenly the weather mattered little. Suddenly it was a good day.

Another goat hunt that springs to mind happened about six months after I came to Waihau.

The large-bodied billy goat was a dark and indistinct shape against a lightening sky when I first saw him, his black horns outlined dramatically. I crouched down, waiting for the light to grow stronger. How would I fare this time, I wondered, for this was the second time I'd come across this particular billy …

The first time had been a month back at a time when I was on the lookout for a deer in rugged country close to the Kaweka Range. He appeared all at once — a jet-black goat coming from thick growth and on to a grassy-topped hillock.

With a good spread of horn a goat can be an impressive trophy.

He was a good way off, maybe as much as three hundred yards, but I felt he was a fine trophy instantly. I'd been wrong before on that count and might be again, for judging trophies on the hoof is like judging distance. I watched him feeding for a short time and then decided there was only one way to really find out how good he was.

Once I was in the scrub proper I headed directly towards the billy. There was no need to worry about being seen, I told myself, for the manuka canopy was at least twelve feet high. Nor was the soft and slight breeze anything to worry about either. But when I reached that open hillock the jet-black goat was gone. Now I was about to get a second chance, something which doesn't happen too frequently with wild animals. As I waited, the light gathered strength quickly. I raised my rifle and looked through the battered Pecar scope. The goat was still and, taking a deep breath, I aimed at his chest.

Range? No more than sixty yards. Easy. Hold bang-on.

Then the goat suddenly dipped his head, moved forward with his head still down, and was gone.

I soon spotted him once more, this time blending into the dark shadows below a low ridge: too chancy to risk a shot. I played the waiting game, so much a part of hunting. And as I waited a soft drawn-out bleat drifted on the still air from beyond the ridge above the billy.

Probably a kid, I thought. So I kept still, knowing how acute a goat's hearing can be. Twin thumps — that's what I heard next. And I knew that the billy I was after, or possibly another, had hit the ground hard with a front hoof. And that's a danger sign if you're a goat!

Now I had lost whatever advantage I may have held. There came a sharp and carrying whistle, an urgent sound filled with fear. I moved fast now, peering into the grey wall of growing lightness. There was a sudden and frantic scatter as the goats raced up a lightly covered manuka slope to the ridge-top. I could see them all now — blurred shapes, indistinct and nondescript.

Except for the big-horned one, that is; the jet-black one. He and several others paused on the ridge-top, turning towards me as they did. After them I raced, my ragged breathing plainly telling me how unfit I was after a heavy cold.

Stopping on the ridge they'd crossed I spotted them fleeing towards the blackness of a wide belt of towering manuka scrub where it was impossible to stalk. How often had I lost game because of that, I thought ruefully, and squatted down on my worn boot-heels.

After a time I had to smile; a wry one to be sure but still a smile. The experienced deer hunter being outwitted by a goat!

To tie up this chapter I'll go back to the June of 1961 when I was a hunter trainee and the goats weren't anything like the ones I've just written about.

Instructor Don Rush, moving quickly up a steep open ridge way above the Branch River in Marlborough, suddenly halted, turned about, and said in a pained fashion: 'Haven't you jokers seen them yet?'

'Seen what?' grunted Bill Puriri, tiny rivulets of sweat streaming across his dark features.

'Those goats over there!' replied Don a moment later.

We both gazed where Don indicated.

Said Don: 'You'll have to learn to look in this game, y'know ...'

Anyway, Don decided I was just the boy to wipe out these ferocious pests and, with me up front, we all set off.

It turned out that a narrow ravine stopped us from walking right up and patting them on the head. As I knelt down and closed the bolt on a Forestry .303 hollow-point, Don, on my left, whispered, 'Easy does it.'

I must admit that I felt proud of myself. Just imagine — two goats and I'd dropped them with just two shots.

On looking back, however, I was sitting down, the range was certainly no more than forty yards and, to make it real tough, the goats were standing and broadside on ...

Some shooting, all right!

Left: Feral goats are spread throughout New Zealand and are an environmental nightmare.

Backblocks — 1974

Makerikeri

One of New Zealand's favourite birds, the tui, renowned for
its amazing vocalisations, can even imitate human speech.

D irectly across the deep valley of the Ikawetea Stream and westwards reared a huge and relatively short landmark — the Otupae Range. To the right and more northerly, where the scrub belt tapered out into cultivated pastures dotted with numerous white woolly specks, were the tempting back reaches of Pohokura outstation; a prime spot for deer poachers these days.

Yet it was neither of these that riveted my attention right then. Instead, my eyes swept over a vast expanse of rolling tussock broken only by outcrops of limestone — the little-known and well tucked away country behind Mangaohane and Otupae stations.

There was Te Rakinuiakura, standing out sharply on this cloudy day. Known to all deer cullers and station hands as Black Hill it climbed well above the Mangaohane plateau country like an enormous and brooding sentinel.

East of that was the tail-end of Ohutu ridge, while across a long stretch of comparatively flattish country was Ruahine Corner hut. Much closer than that was another hut, one I think back on with a great deal of affection, nostalgia, and anything else a sentimental fool is capable of: Makerikeri.

I turned to Bill Nikl, for this was the time we had left Bill's car at No Mans hut for an overnight stay, and said: 'Ever spend any time at Makerikeri, Bill?'

Bill shook his head slowly. 'Just once with Peter Cook, that's all. Would have liked to, though, from what I've heard. Must have been mighty there.' Then he looked away and his arm swept and settled down below where we rested. 'See that long, narrow clearing?'

I nodded.

'That's where I shot my best red stag on the job — a lousy eight-pointer.' He shook his head sorrowfully. 'Not much to show for all those years culling.'

Bill stood up and shouldered into his lightweight Mountain Mule pack. And then we were off, heading along the main Ruahine Range until we could drop down to the edge of farm country where, Bill told me, was a broken-down and smoky hut and where, better still, we were sure to see a fair number of red deer.

The man was right on both counts.

But it wasn't the deer that really made that trip. No, it was the sight of that wonderful Mangaohane country, the place where I finished up my time as a deer culler; where the hunting was so much better than anywhere else; where there sits a hut in a well-hidden hollow called Makerikeri …

It was raining hard when I closed the door of Ruahine Corner hut; mist clung tenaciously to the grasslands and blotted out anything beyond one hundred yards. Cold with it, too. It was October, 1967, a few weeks after the start of the summer hunting season in the Ruahine Range.

Soon the mist was all about me, rising and falling in slow motion. Mist. Rain. And soaking grass swishing unpleasantly against my bare legs. A day to be sitting before a good fire and turning the pages of a paperback. But I'd made up my mind I was going to Makerikeri the previous day and, well, that was that.

Anyway, what was mist and rain and cold to a deer culler or high-country musterer? He learnt to live with such things, to accept the harsh conditions for what they were. It's a wise man who bends before a strong wind.

I had walked this way yesterday morning, hunting around to the Scar — a distinct landmark where the topsoil had long since vanished. Shot four deer as the sun climbed behind me and turned a world of nondescript grey into one

Home for the musterer, the possum hunter, the deer culler: that's Makerikeri hut.

of brilliant colour. Did the same thing in the evening, too. Only on the lower slopes of Black Hill this time. Eight deer. Not bad for 1967. At $3.60 a tail. But remembering how it had seemed here yesterday morning, I might have been somewhere else entirely.

Fortunately the rain had slackened off somewhat, while the mist, if anything, was even denser. Just as well my sense of direction was working as it should, I thought. Otherwise I might have ended up doing what I'd done before more than once — walked in a complete circle!

With the hut only thirty minutes away at the most now, the mist suddenly began to rise, revealing a sloping patch of green and well-cropped grass surrounded by tall tussock and a few patches of straggling scrub. And …

Seven deer, too. Heads down. About 150 yards away. I'd thought before that it was time I saw something at this particular spot and now I had.

Kneeling down, I removed my pack and unzipped my parka and took out a small plastic bag from a shirt pocket. It contained a piece of chamois cloth and a tight wad of tissue — Forestry issue toilet paper in other words. Using the chamois cloth first, I cleaned the rain splattered and fogged-up scope lens.

As so often happens the rising mist was only a temporary thing — an illusion which might never have been. Still, that could work for me. Perhaps they'd be unable to wind me, because thick mist has always seemed to have a definite deadening effect — noise, scent, everything. And certainly they'd be unable to see me!

Leaving the pack where it was, I angled to higher ground for a short distance and then cut directly towards the deer. Seven deer, I was thinking. How many would I be able to get in conditions like this? One? Two? Perhaps three if I was real lucky. Maybe none!

Weka, with their curious nature, can often be found round the campsite.

All at once there was a red deer hind right in front of me, and by her side a yearling. Both feeding. The others, I knew, would be close. They might as well have been miles away.

It was two at the very most.

The hind, as always, first. Damn! The scope lens had fogged up again. I should have checked before.

'Woof!' went the hind; an oddly hollow sound, yet somehow flattened out by the heavy mist so that the distance it carried would be small. When a deer does that one thing's for real: something has upset it.

In this case the answer was rather obvious — me!

And I was desperately wiping the front scope lens clean of moisture.

'Woof!' went the hind again.

Then it was my turn to say something. And I let the .243 do the speaking.

She flopped down to a neck shot and the yearling leapt away, the mist its saviour, for I saw and heard nothing of it or the others again. Still, I mused, taking the hind's tail, one was a whole lot better than the way it could easily have turned out.

Before reaching Makerikeri hut, a cut track takes you through belts of heavy scrub interspersed by truly beautiful clearings. In spring and early summer, or after a solid downpour, these are a fine spot to find a sika or red deer.

Today there was nothing. Nothing but a decomposing heap of skinned possums — white and obscene — which damn near made me gag as I passed close to them.

Five minutes later I was cutting down a steep bank to the Makerikeri Stream, and, once across, there it was: Makerikeri hut. And here, just briefly, I'll describe it.

Its sides were lined with malthoid, its roof tin; its chimney a manuka-poled and tin affair. There were three bunks inside, the floor was dirt which had been trampled into rock-like consistency over the years; a single window hung on by a leather strap, a wooden table wobbled on two unsteady legs: mice were there in plenty, the odd rat, too, and possums played on the roof at night.

It was Makerikeri — a station hut — and I've never stayed in a hut I've liked more.

I pushed open the unsteady door and went inside. It was fairly clean inside. There was some dry manuka brush and kindling stacked near the fireplace, a large amount of manuka logs outside. The hard and unreasonable way I'd been feeling about the possum hunter melted. I lit a fire, half filled a small billy and hung it to a long wire hook. Then I changed into dry gear which, of course, made me feel so much better.

While waiting for the water to boil, I checked on the food supply. There were no miceproof cupboards here. Instead, tinned stuff was left in cartons shoved under the bunks, and everything else in flour-bins. The total sum came to something like this: a dozen tins of rusty sweet corn; nearly a full tin of instant coffee; ample sugar and tea; several half-used packets of porridge; some smelly butter and fat partly covered with grey-looking flour thick with lumps and the odd bit of mice dirt.

This was what a man was supposed to start the season on; to hang on until the next airdrop which, I'd been told by my boss, Henry Dorrian, was to take place early in the new year. Great!

Oh, I was forgetting. There was a full packet of rusks which the possum hunter must have left. So what was I moaning about?

On the credit side, there was ample kerosene and candles. It's a pity the lamp was no good!

Anyway, I took a bite of the baby food and considered my position. Obviously, I thought, there wasn't enough to keep me going here. Ruahine Corner hut was better stocked, although not as I'd have liked to see it. The other huts — Remutupo and Colenso — were fine, even if what was there was rather old. There was no other way: I'd have to pack some food from there, because it was here I wanted to stay, here where a man could shoot double figures in a single day with a bit of luck.

Then a name came to my mind — Ikawetea hut. Ikawetea Forks hut, really. Hell, that was no distance away. I dug out a Lands and Survey map from my pack and found it; a hut right where the Ikawetea Stream forked, naturally enough.

I'd never been there while hunting the North-Eastern block in 1963 and, from what I'd heard recently, it was still pretty much alone. This was easy to understand from a hunter's angle, for the hut was surrounded by heavy bush, mainly beech, where the hunting was tough. Certainly the animals were there, but they were far easier to get when they came up on to the Mangaohane Plateau country. Apart from this, a man had to face a stiff climb using the hut, unless he went downstream and hunted the faces of the Ikawetea. Not a good scene, whichever way you consider it.

So, if the hut wasn't being used much, maybe this would be the answer. And there was only one way of finding out …

Rain was again my companion the following morning as I cut down a steep bush face to the Ikawetea Stream. My pack was empty but I had high hopes it wouldn't be that way on the return trip.

It was quicker than I thought to reach the stream, which was churning along in great style after the rain of late — more of a river really. Still, I had no trouble crossing

it several times until, on a high bank, I reached the hut. Ikawetea Forks hut turned out to be one of the more recent Forestry jobs: big and roomy six-bunk affairs. Mice scuttled away as I entered. The inside felt cold and damp; unlived in.

Unlike Forest Service huts in more recent times, there was no lock on the door. I unbolted it and knew then how Aladdin must have felt when he saw the treasure-filled cave. For this was a treasure too. Treasure in the way of tinned fruit of several kinds; tins of sweet biscuits, instant coffee, salmon, corned beef; almost everything you could possibly expect to find in a Forestry hut. I'd never seen such a well-stocked food cupboard since the early sixties, back when there was no financial squeeze on the department to tighten its belt.

I looked at it again: bloody marvellous! I'd live like a king now at Makerikeri with the best of hunting and the best of food to go with it. I moved a few tins of fruit out of the way and a row of instant puddings stared back; tins of egg powder, rice.

While waiting for the fire to get a spurt on, I quickly thumbed back through the pages of the visitors' book. There were so few entries over the years that Ikawetea Forks hut must have been the most neglected in the country. The last entry, some time back, told me I was looking at what I'd suspected — a full airdrop which hadn't been touched. As yet!

As well as this wonderful find, there was a carton filled with magazines and a few paperbacks, including an Evan Hunter I hadn't read. It was a mighty happy hunter who staggered back to Makerikeri hut that wet October day.

All in all I was to make four trips to Ikawetea Forks hut before we finally received an airdrop, and I never felt bad about it, for even then there was plenty left. And even if I was on a different block, it was meant for deer cullers. Leastways, that's what I always told myself when filling my pack.

All through that spring the hunting was really something at Makerikeri and, later on, the nearby Otupae Range was the place to sleep out. But it's the hut itself which seems to stay more in my mind than the hunting I enjoyed there; that and something else which has nothing at all to do with deer …

One evening I was following the Makerikeri Stream back to the hut, the usual thing to do if you've been hunting the bush-clad slopes of the Otupae Range. I had almost reached the hut when, out of the corner of my eye, I spotted a morepork perched on the dead branch of a once healthy tree. In the gloom of the closed-in stream, and because of the bird's dark colouring, I nearly missed seeing it. Surprisingly there was no move on its part to fly off and I looked at it with delight, for our small brown owl is one of my favourite birds.

Slowly, I moved a little closer. Then a bit more. And still the morepork stayed put — a dark brown bundle of feathers with those huge yellow saucers for eyes.

Now only six feet or so separated us and here I came to a full stop; I'd pushed my luck hard enough already. We eyed each other for maybe two minutes and then I went on my way. It had been a completely unexpected incident and one that put me in a carefree sort of mood.

Several days later — and in the same spot again — I saw it once more. This time, however, it flew up on to that same branch from lower down; from a well-concealed hollow where the roots of two large trees met. A casual glance would never have seen this fern-covered spot. But I understood the reason why the morepork was reluctant to leave when I carefully parted the ferns — two white eggs in

Fallow deer fawn.

a rather crude nest. I moved on quickly then, not wanting to disturb the bird any more.

Two weeks passed and then I returned to Makerikeri after spending some time at the other huts on the block. That same day I checked on the nest. There was no adult bird present, just two chicks dressed in a thick white down. They were so small and helpless I felt my heart go out to them.

From then on I would go to the nest nearly every day. Sometimes there were two adult birds there; so it would seem that the old man was doing his bit too. And the really big thing, where I was concerned, was that they seemed to know I meant no danger; that they even seemed to accept me. And that was a real good feeling.

The two-week Christmas break loomed up and it was well into the new year before I was able to look into the nest again. This time it was empty and I went back to the hut both disappointed and sad: my little harmless friends of such short acquaintance were gone.

Backblocks — 1974

Take a Rest, Friend

A group of hinds and their fawns.

Fawn.

To the east of the Kaweka Range, beyond a scrub-strangled valley where Lotkow hut stands, is the Don Juan Range. The tops of this are mainly bare, shingle-like rock and patches of clay where the tracks of deer stand out clearly. The highest point of the Don Juan is a mere 2091 feet, and all in all it's pretty much dominated by the overpowering Kawekas in the background.

Down from these rocky tops there is an abundance of native bush and, of course, the inevitable scrub one never really seems to get away from. And it was here — one fine June day in 1973 — that I saw one of the biggest boars I'd ever seen.

He was a gingery sort of fellow, short-legged, with most of his weight typically up front. Best of all, though, he wasn't aware of me, being snout down amid some low fern and grunting happily to himself. At this stage I'd had an unbroken string of one-shot kills and, because of this, I must have become over-confident in my ability, for the rifle was to my shoulder in a flash, a shot fired; and that's the last I saw of that particular boar. There's a lesson here — and one I'll emphasise even further.

There were two of us that long-ago day — two tired and hungry cullers coming down from the lofty mist-clad tops after three and a half weeks of shooting deer, eating deer and, to judge by my mate, smelling like deer too. Two cullers, I'll add, who never really got along like most two-man teams did. It wasn't his fault, it wasn't mine; it just proved that a person can't get along with everybody.

Then suddenly — and almost straight below — we were overlooking a tiny, grassy basin that nestled rather snugly below an overhanging rock of considerable size. There was a tarn here — a minute patch of vivid blue reflecting the day in glorious fashion amidst the off-yellow brown of the tussock. Better still, to go by the expression on my mate's in-need-of-a-shave face, was the sight of a red stag. A red stag basking in the sun. We both crouched down at once. We didn't speak, for a man's voice, even when pitched low, can travel a long distance in open country.

The stag had a fine-looking head, which rather surprised me, for you rarely see such good antler development on red deer east of the Ruahine Range. West of it, too, come to that.

It had been previously arranged that the other half of our two-man party would have a crack at the next deer we came across and, in those days, one did come across deer at regular intervals. And this antlered beauty — blast it all — was it! Mine, back up the long ridge, had been a runty sort of spiker. You know the type, I'm sure: two long spikes about a foot in length and only good for toasting bread.

Still, I wasn't really too upset, for I'd known it wasn't going to be my day since I'd tried my mate's wonderful recipe for burnt porridge. Glancing sideways, I saw he wasn't doing anything but gape. I could understand that; he'd most likely never seen a stag like this.

'Come on,' I breathed into his ear. 'He won't stay there forever, you know.' I often come up with gems like that.

The sound of my voice brought him from his slightly dazed state into wild, sudden and thoughtless action. He flung off his pack and raised his cannon in a movement too quick to really follow. Next second, it seemed, there was an almighty blast in my left ear which meant he'd fired a shot. I also noted that he'd shot from the upright position.

From the way the stag leapt into the air the shot must have gone very close, maybe right below his belly. Actually, the stag put me in mind of a chopper taking off.

Back on the ground once more the stag lumbered away and another shot from my left ripped up the sod some two or three yards behind him and urged him on at a faster pace than ever. A moment later, and just when I was thinking of joining in, he was out of sight, the white tips of his fine antlers showing last of all.

Turning to me, his face woeful in the extreme, old crackshot moaned: 'Oh, how mighty those antlers would have looked at home. There's a spot just right for them above the fireplace.' He paused and booted a clump of tussock hard. 'Now how did I miss two such easy shots?' Once more his boot was in action, kicking the poor clump to death.

I had a damn good idea how he felt and would normally have been sympathetic. But I was never really myself with this guy and I scoffed: 'Call them easy, d'you. Why, that stag was all of eighty yards away at the very least — maybe a bit more. Reckon I'd have missed as well …'

'You know,' he thoughtfully mused a moment later and I gave him a Robert Mitchum look, uplifted brows and all that, and he went on. 'It's no wonder I missed out really — I was shaking like a goddam leaf!'

'Yeah, it happens,' I agreed in a more relenting tone. Then I stated the obvious: 'Didn't you even think of taking a rest of some sort?'

He frowned and shook his head sadly.

'Not at the time, no. I suppose I could have knelt down, come to that.' And his voice, sadder than ever, trailed away into nothing.

But smart old me wouldn't let it go there.

'Too right you could. In fact, you could've used your pack — rested your rifle on that rock over there. Even sat

Philip Holden amongst typical beech forest, taking aim in a sound shooting position.

on your arse. Anything but the upright position.' I raised my eyebrows at him again in what was sure to have been an annoying way. 'How long have you been hunting anyway?'

He stooped down and picked up his bulky pack. 'Get stuffed,' he said shortly, shouldering into it.

'My next shot,' I flashed back at him.

'Like bloody hell!' he called over his shoulder, for he was already off, making sure he was in front when it was really my turn to lead the way. All the same I let him go; it paid to keep the peace when you had to live in one room with a man and, besides, I'd have been feeling a bit like him had I missed such a fine stag.

The only time one shoots upright and unaided is when there is no other choice — that's right out of the professional's book — because there is nothing like taking support of some kind to ensure a quick and a clean kill. And that, I reckon, is something we should all aim for.

It's a fact that you'll never see a really knowing man blazing away without some kind of aid unless, of course, he's reacted to the situation in a way he normally wouldn't do — as I did with the gingery boar. Still, if there's one thing I've learnt about hunting and hunters, it's this: a man will never stop making mistakes, and for the simple reason that the human element is involved.

There are many times, of course, when a man has to shoot as fast as he can or forget all about it. This is especially true in bush or scrub country. Yet it's been my experience that a man will often have ample time to look

The rabbit, a serious pest to New Zealand, makes for good target practice.

around for a rest of some kind — a pack is fine if one is packing at the time. A pack, I've found, makes the very best of rests in open country. Another thing, I usually sight-in my rifle with the help of a pack — with a tightly rolled sleeping bag inside. Then a rock might be handy, a gentle rise, a log. And if there's absolutely nothing, a man can always kneel or, better still, sit down. Both these positions allow the shooter far more room to move than does the prone position. Running game will be far easier to handle, and reloading and getting back on to the target will be quicker. All these things add up.

It's a different story in heavy bush. I've never got down on my stomach among the beech trees and I suspect no one else has either. Still, you never know.

Even so, I still try for a rest whenever possible. Mostly I find there's time enough to sit down, time also to settle the rifle's stock over a nearby log. I've often rested the rifle up against a tree trunk to pull off a rather tricky shot which, without that rest, I'd have most likely missed.

I've frequently come across game of all sorts that were ready to spring away because they'd spotted or winded me. The first impulse is to fire — and as fast as possible. It's an entirely natural reaction, I guess. Yet in the majority of cases I've found they'll stay around long enough for you to find that vital rest; and with that rest you're more than halfway there.

All action and no thought has never been a winning combination in the hunting game …

The Deer Hunters — 1976

Incident with a Sika Stag

In the Ripia River country: Tom Condon looks towards Big Ben
(3602 feet), which is well known to have numerous sika.

A young sika stag in mid April. It was perhaps an hour after first light when I spotted him. The dense manuka scrub belt, so favoured by this species, is but a few short bounds away and that is exactly where this fine fellow ended up.

To hunter Brian Burdon the word sika conjures up the most vicious, mean-tempered and ornery brutes likely to be encountered in the New Zealand wilds.

I first met Brian in Kaweka country in early '62. We were culling at the time under ranger Morrie Robson. Brian had recently come up from the South Island where he'd been contract shooting on an extremely tough block. He's a ruggedly built character a little below average height, as are many who have hunted professionally in this country, although height has nothing to do with one's hunting ability.

Brian's an extremely witty type, that rare kind of wit which is never cruel. Add to this a sharp sense of humour and you end up with the very best kind of companion to be stuck with in a crappy sort of hut on a likewise sort of day.

During his time in the Kaweka Range, Brian became a top-flight bush hunter. He was particularly effective on sika; he'd deliberately hunted the places where sika were likely to be found, the scrubby foothills around the Lawrence and Lotkow huts, and I think it's safe to say that Brian ended up shooting more sika than any other professional hunter in the Kawekas.

A story of Brian's about sika I particularly like had as a background a freezing day in early May, 1965, when Brian was travelling along the crest of the Black Birch Range with a mate, Geoff Beale (a long-time culler in the Kawekas who had finished hunting professionally but had returned for the six-week 'roar', a sort of working holiday on full pay, according to Geoff). That holiday was almost over, for they were making tracks out to the hunters' base camp at Kuripapango.

Fresh snow lay on the Black Birch Range, covering the open ground to about eight inches in depth and perhaps

Philip Holden in the Ikawetea Valley, 1979.

The sika deer is a highly vocal species, with over 10 individual sounds ranging from soft whistles to loud screams.

three inches less in the bush. Directly to the west the main Kaweka Range loomed large, its topmost parts well covered with snow. The hunters had just reached one of the many clearings amid the overwhelming scrub when Brian stopped; one of his puttees had come loose and was trailing by the yard behind him.

'Won't be a minute, Geoff.'

Geoff nodded. He was feeling the cold as bitterly as he ever had and was more than anxious to get moving. And right then, while Brian was retying his puttee, a sika stag appeared on the Christmas-like scene, about 30 yards distant; a snorting sika stag at the peak of the rutting time. Both hunters' eyes boggled.

Geoff hissed urgently. 'Better get him. I've nothin' in the mag …'

And still the stag stood there, eyeing them defiantly, making a splendid sight as snorts of white vapour jetted from his flared nostrils and evaporated in the chill, almost brittle, air.

Brian was fumbling with the seemingly frozen bolt of his rifle, his numb hands sticking to the frozen metal.

'The bloody round won't feed in,' he croaked huskily. And he took a fast look at the stag.

Right on the dot, as if Brian's glance had been its cue, the stag began to prance forward, with a stiff-legged, menacing gait.

Geoff whistled, an almost sure ploy to halt any deer, especially a stag as worked up as was this one. But for once it didn't work. Geoff's piercing whistle, which would have had many a shepherd's dogs cringing at his heels, acted as a direct challenge to the stag. Or that's how the enraged animal wanted to interpret it. It suddenly lowered its head and charged …

Both Brian and Geoff have told me this story many times, Brian when first they arrived at the base camp the same day looking like two frozen zombies. I could visualise the complete scene: on a snow-topped range, the sika stag leaping towards them, his sharp-tipped weapons lowered in a fighting position, Geoff with nothing in the magazine of his rifle, his hands probably too cold to do anything about it anyway, and Brian fumbling desperately to get a round into the breech of his rifle.

Then, with a mere 20 feet separating hunters and stag, the stag came to an abrupt, propping halt, almost as though he'd come to the end of a fully taut tether. At this point Brian finally got that cursed round where he wanted it, and taking a lightning-fast bead, fired.

The shot was true, the stag dropped. As it did, a sika hind scampered away from where the defiant stag had first appeared. Both hunters were quick to the fallen sika. He was dead. His thick coat was winter-dark, his antlers well shaped and of eight points. The hunters looked at each other and grinned hugely. They agreed that a man never quite knows what will happen next in sika country.

The Deer Hunters — 1976

Moose Means a
Question Mark

*A wide variety of ferns, trees and shrubs flourishes in this
typical rainforest, in the upper valley of the Arthur River.*

Imagine, if you can, a hunter's feelings on abruptly coming face to face with a deer, possibly standing six feet six inches at the shoulder, weighing as much as fifteen hundred pounds, and that might possess antlers spanning as much as 6½ feet! Such a confrontation would, I'm sure, be equally daunting to both hunter and bull moose.

In the case of the hunter, even though his fanciful dreams might have included meeting up with such a giant, it could well be the last thing he'd expect to see; even if he were deliberately looking for one.

And the bull moose — well, he wouldn't in all probability have winded a man before. So, man and moose would start off pretty much on the same footing. The moose, one expects, would somehow sense an enemy for he, being truly of the wild, would have an inbuilt instinct for such things and would lumber away with that peculiar moose gait; a long-stepping affair if ever there was one.

The hunter — most likely so flattened by surprise he wouldn't know what to do — might still realise that if he did manage to shoot the bull he'd bring off the hunting coup of the year, or any other year. It's been done before, of course, though it was over twenty years ago.

I have always been deeply interested when hunters' talk has switched to moose, and the story of moose in New Zealand is intriguing. In either late 1900 or early 1901, fourteen moose were obtained by the New Zealand Acclimatisation Society from the Hudson Bay Trading Company, Canada, and duly shipped. Unfortunately, the ship ran into foul weather between Vancouver and Honolulu;

Clinton Valley, Fiordland National Park.

weather, it was reported, which lashed and battered the ship without mercy. When the storm passed, it was found that ten of the moose either had died or were injured to such degree they had to be destroyed, only two bulls and two cows surviving. Truly a major disaster for those sponsoring the first attempt to introduce moose in reasonable numbers.

Reports conflict about the fate of those moose which survived. The most likely outcome was that the bulls and one of the cows somehow found their way into the Hokitika Gorge. The bulls were seen about a year later and then never again. The cow was spotted several times in the next year and then she, too, was seen no more. Perhaps the moose were shot for meat. Perhaps they died of natural causes.

But by all accounts the second cow settled in the back of Doughboy, near Vine Creek. There she lived for some fourteen years before she either died a natural death or was shot. For most of the time she made a great nuisance of herself so far as the local settlers were concerned.

The next attempt to settle moose in New Zealand took place in 1907. The Acclimatisation Society was again fortunate that the Canadian Government relaxed their strict regulations regarding export of the animals, and four bulls and six cows left Canada.

All arrived here safely, even though they experienced temperatures of 90 degrees while travelling through the tropics. They were set free at Supper Cove, south-west Fiordland. It seems certain the choice of this part of the country was made so they would encounter little in the way of human activity while establishing themselves.

When one considers the area in which the moose were released, with its precipitous terrain and its rainfall (which exceeds 200 inches a year), the choice was hardly an inspired one. Even at the time many people openly regarded the choice of south-west Fiordland as madness. Only the hardiest and most adaptable deer could survive there — and moose were a long way from being in that category. This had already been proved in failed attempts to transplant moose from higher to lower latitudes in North America. The most telling experiment of all was that no moose had ever managed to survive in the New York zoo. This zoo has a latitude of 40 degrees north. South-west Fiordland is 45 degrees south.

However, in 1912 a mining party discovered sure evidence of moose in Dusky Sound. Other reports filtered through from time to time, and all strongly indicated that the moose were alive and well. A government investigator went into the moose country in 1921 and came out with wonderful news; he'd actually seen live moose.

Two years later the first hunting licences were issued. Speculation about the size of the antlers the bulls would produce were rife. Perhaps they would rank alongside those which the moose of North America produce. Antlers of such size and weight as would stagger the imagination.

Despite many attempts by hunters, all incredibly keen to account for the first bull moose to be shot in the Southern Hemisphere, it was six years later in 1929 that it was first achieved. The elated hunter was E. J. Herrick. The bull had

The first moose shot in New Zealand, by E. J. Herrick; the hunter and his trophy. (Auckland Weekly News)

five points on each side, a spread of 39⅞ inches, but little palmation. It was far from trophy class but, even so, it added up to an important first.

The same Mr Herrick, who must have been a remarkable and persistent hunter, accounted for the second bull moose five years later. The antlers this time were better, having thirteen points overall and a spread of 36 inches; the palmation was also superior. In addition, Herrick shot a badly diseased cow.

In the next seventeen years no moose were shot; nor were they reportedly seen. They might, it would seem, have ceased to exist. This period is one of confusion. Rumour had it that moose had been shot along the Fiordland coastline.

If this was fact, then the reason for not openly reporting the kills could have been that those who were responsible thought they had committed a punishable offence. That might have been the case before 1934, but since that year moose have been removed from the protected list. Another possibility is that these 'moose', if there were any, might have been wapiti. It is a highly likely supposition because anyone unfamiliar with both species could mistake one animal for the other.

How the moose were truly faring intrigued a great many men. In 1950, two hunters, Maxwell Curtis and R. V. Francis-Smith, resolved to find out in the only possible way. They made an overland trip from Lake Manapouri to the Seaforth Valley, experiencing bad weather, nothing new for the area of course. They were of the opinion that there were no moose in the Seaforth Valley or any of its arms above Lake Maree.

The same men returned a year later with another hunter, P. J. Lyes, who was keen to learn about the moose and their survival.

Lyes was a government hunter who, two years before, had shot what was then (and still is, from all I've been able to gather) the New Zealand record for red deer antler length. He shot this fourteen-pointer in the Hokitika Valley. The right antler measured 50 inches, the left 47½ inches. Measurements like those make one think of a wapiti and not a red deer.

On the trip of 1951 the hunters covered all the lower Seaforth Valley and right up to the head of the Long Burn — the Hauroko Burn — and country running through to Wet Jacket Arm. Only one moose, a cow, was seen. They estimated that the moose in this area, most likely contained in the country bordering Wet Jacket Arm, numbered thirty animals. They found old tracks of moose near Supper Cove and in the heads of Bishop Burn. They also found the skeletons of four cows and one young bull, all long dead.

The following year, in April 1952, the trio returned to Wet Jacket Arm. This time Percy Lyes shot the best moose ever taken in New Zealand. It was also the last. The eight-tined antlers had an overall spread of 45¾ inches, a palmation of 5½ inches. While these antlers fall far short of those taken overseas, they must still rank as one of the best deer trophies ever to be shot here. They estimated the weight of the bull was in the vicinity of twelve hundred pounds. They also measured the bull's height from hoof to wither —

6½ feet. When one considers that Percy Lyes shot this bull, and also the red stag I mentioned above, it certainly puts him in an enviable position as a hunter. Apart from the highlight of the trip, they also saw two young bulls and one cow, all seemingly in top condition. It's to the hunters' credit that they left them alone.

In January 1955, a young Internal Affairs hunter named Keith Purdon was in south-west Fiordland. With him were Max Kershaw, Allan Aikne and Philip Dorizac. Their job was to rebuild a hut at Supper Cove. Purdon was fired with the possibility of shooting a bull moose and one day went off to explore a side-creek of Supper Cove itself — a distance of about one mile. It was here that he stumbled across the remains of a dead cow moose, partly covered by huge ferns. Using the barrel of his cut-down .303, he judged her shoulder height at around 5 feet 8 inches.

Later, in another side-creek which joined Supper Cove, he saw a high browse-line, eight, maybe nine feet above the ground. That was too high for any red deer to reach, and the answer was obvious: moose. There were old, scuffed tracks there too, definitely made by moose. To Keith they appeared about the size an average two-year-old Jersey bull would make, but were naturally deer-shaped.

In May of '65, Keith Purdon returned to Dusky Sound. He was alone this time and had given himself twelve days to find one thing — a bull moose. He set off with company. The company was Ric, a male Blue Heeler which was crossed somewhere along the line. To some men, and understandably, a dog is the best of all company in the hills. For men like Keith, the prospect of living alone and rough in country as wild and remote as south-west Fiordland held no secret fears. He had that supreme, unshakable confidence in

The mighty Earland Falls. Fiordland National Park.

his own ability which comes from the life he knew so well as a deer culler; tough, lonely, but deeply rewarding.

He had joined the Internal Affairs Department in '48 when, following the long Second World War years with most of the country's riflemen overseas, deer were to be found in uncountable numbers. Keith had joined the Department on Stewart Island, along with his good friend, Harry Vipond. Together, they had a great time hunting what was then a little-known species of deer, whitetail. Now they are both senior environmental rangers, Harry Vipond for the Rotorua Conservancy, and Keith Purdon based in Auckland.

Beginning his hunt Keith crossed the Chisholm Burn, then the Bishop, and then a burn he's now unsure of. From there he crossed in to a side-creek of Wet Jacket Arm. Red deer were everywhere he looked! Thin, stunted in growth, docile; a veritable plague of red deer.

At this time, red deer here had possibly never heard a rifle shot. With no control by man, and a total lack of predators to thin their ranks, they had just multiplied until they'd reached locust-like proportions. A true example of red deer left completely unmolested. They were no good, not even to themselves.

One fourteen-pointer Keith shot was in such a rundown condition that its antlers had reached a length of only 20 inches and had a spread of less than half that.

It's well worth writing here about red deer in this area, for they have played a vital part in keeping moose numbers so low. Red deer were released in south-west Fiordland in 1909 and peak populations are now considered to have been reached between the years 1945–60. Since then they have declined in numbers, following a general depletion of palatable vegetation, but even taking into account the

A rare picture of live bull moose, Seaforth River, Fiordland, 1928.

L. Murrell

staggering numbers brought out by helicopter shooters, there are still more deer here than anywhere else in the country. And since red deer favour the same kind of country as moose in which to feed — clearings, sunny faces, etc. — competition between the two has not helped the moose.

Red deer browse heavily as well as graze. They are able to utilise any available feed and they forage better than a moose. This might sound odd, for a moose is far taller than a red deer. Yet there is a noticeable lack of suitable vegetation above the height red deer are able to reach, meaning the moose's extra height isn't much of an advantage when browsing.

Once Keith Purdon was in Wet Jacket Arm proper, he headed upstream until he came to a well-hidden lake gleaming amid a jungle of ribbonwood trees. Red deer were thick. Bark had been ripped off most of the trees, low-hanging vegetation was non-existent. While getting some handy venison for himself and Ric, Keith saw something which brought him to a full stop: a high-browse line. Moose, was the thought which flashed through his excited mind.

He scouted but was unable to find anything which proved moose were around. Later, when rechecking, he found droppings about the size of a ten-cent piece. They were fairly old. He pressed on further towards the heads of the tributaries of Wet Jacket Arm. There was no sign of moose there, only of red deer. He returned to the ribbonwood-surrounded lake and there, skirting the lower and shallow end of the lake, he saw fresh moose droppings.

He knelt beside the absolute proof and picked one up. It was longish and shaped like that which a wapiti would drop. It felt warm but he knew that the sun could be an explanation for that. Even so, he was sure it had been dropped overnight.

Ric, Keith noticed, was sniffing the air excitedly. But he was always doing that with so many red deer around. 'C'mon, Ric,' he said softly. 'Let's find us a moose.' And Ric followed him.

Every step Keith took was a slow one; his eyes checked every piece of ground, every tree. And there, way up there, was a wineberry sapling, two or three inches in diameter,

freshly browsed to a height of at least 18 feet. Keith knew the largest of all deer would straddle such a tree and use his weight to bring it down to feeding level. With Ric's help he tracked the moose across open ground into forested country. There the tracks and the moose's scent, judging by Ric's attitude, vanished.

But the hunt was not over yet. He would stay another two days before leaving the area, otherwise a search party would be looking for him … He was right out of luck; it rained solidly throughout the two days.

The moose story leaps ahead to 1972. A forest research team was put ashore on a stony beach well up Wet Jacket Arm. Their objective was to find moose. One of the four men who watched the *Miss Akaroa* ease away from the beach with a gentle swish of white-capped water was Ken Tustin. I first met him in the Kaweka mountains in 1963. At the time I was camped with a fellow culler, Geoff Beale, at Kiwi Mouth hut. Ken and a friend turned up on a hunting trip. He was then seventeen years old. When next I bumped into Ken, at Te Anau four years later, he'd shot up and filled out too — it was hard to recognise him as that teenager I'd met in the mountains in the North Island. At Te Anau he was working with a forestry research team on a survey of wapiti. Since then he has picked up a BSc degree in zoology and a BSF wildlife management degree which the University of British Columbia hands out to those who rate it.

Rain was falling as the *Miss Akaroa* departed and the four men started to shift two hundred man-days of stores away from the tide to a spot which would give temporary shelter. This was to be their base camp and one of four sites they would operate from during the next two and a half months. This was no haphazard expedition, but the most concentrated attempt yet made to find out about moose in this country.

The survey, or to be more correct, reconnaissance, was to be limited to areas where past records proved moose had existed. It would include all the many arms of Dusky Sound, the Seaforth Valley, Wet Jacket Arm, and all the major parts of Resolution, Long and Cooper Islands. These areas would be checked over more than once, usually by parties of two or three men. Difficult waterways would be handled with dinghy and outboard motor.

A full, tiring month passed without any sign of moose. Then came a breakthrough; a high browse-line which seemed to have been made the previous season. It gave the hunters a great boost, for morale had been flagging.

Yet another full month was to pass before any further sign was found. The party had been in the area a full nine weeks — and nine sodden weeks at that. It was now April and, in a spot they'd checked before, fresh sign was found. It spurred them on and for the next five days they combed the area relentlessly; a rough stretch of forest perhaps three-quarters of a mile square. The weather was against them; rain and strong variable winds carried their smell in every direction. Even so, they managed to disturb an animal on several occasions. They found where it had bedded down, where it had browsed, and where it had backtracked on them. The moose, it seemed, might have been looking them over from a well-hidden spot even while they searched for him!

They failed to sight a live moose on this expedition, but there were compensations which proved moose were still alive. They found droppings which were far too big to be those of red deer. They found hair which didn't belong to a red deer and which later, with the help of a microscope, was positively identified as belonging to a moose. Another prize was the cast antler of a young bull dropped, they thought, several seasons earlier.

How many moose there are in south-west Fiordland was difficult for them to estimate, or hazard a guess. The sign they did come across, and this was found in seven widely scattered areas, suggested between twenty-five and fifty animals.

One positive conclusion they reached was that the moose population in New Zealand, unless given every opportunity to increase its numbers (which is difficult to envisage), faces sure extinction.

The Deer Hunters — 1976

Side to Hunting

J udged from their experiences and the conversations I've had with a number of overseas hunters, there's a side to hunting in New Zealand which is not at all well known; the grim side wherein one man shoots another in mistake for a deer. As once almost happened to me …

The shot suddenly screamed overhead, sounding like a thousand supercharged hornets: a vicious, high, whining scream, so terrifyingly close that for a numbed second or two I was completely incapable of movement. Instinctively I hugged the damp ground. Right then I couldn't think of a better spot.

A few hours earlier I had arrived at Block 10 in the Kawekas. I was about to cross Gorge Stream for the first time when a battered ute growled into sight and parked by my beat-up Viva on the stream's edge.

I went back reluctantly. There were four of them, hunters obviously.

'G'day,' I mumbled. Standard greeting whether you mean it or not.

'G'day yourself,' one replied. He looked about as happy as I felt. Things were becoming a little crowded.

I was soon to point out: 'Far too many blokes being shot in mistake for a deer these days. We'd better work out where everyone's going.'

'My word, yes!' exclaimed one of the four. 'She's a dangerous game and no mistake.'

With a sharp-pointed stick to draw a rough map of the area in the sandy soil, we started to work it out. Fortunately, they all had a fair idea of the country. It was soon clarified and settled. They would be hunting in Block 9 (blocks 9 and 10 more or less joined where we were). That suited me fine. Between the two blocks was a long, sharp-backed spur which eventually finished up on the Don Juan tops.

Off I went once more; the way our plans had been worked out I was still able to hunt where I'd wanted to. But by late evening I hadn't seen a thing. Deer were around yet for all the good that did me they might have been ghosts. Nimble-hoofed ghosts which left freshly slotted tracks in the soft ground. Sika!

Perhaps twenty minutes later I was slowly edging my way through fairly thick manuka, hookgrass tugging without pity at the hairs on my legs. A sneaky nettle brushed softly but potently against my cheek — yes, they grow that high! Then, through the thinning trees, I spotted a red deer feeding in a familiar clearing.

It was then the bullet screamed overhead. Directly overhead. And there I was hugging the ground again.

Twisting my head, I looked towards the clearing. Whoever had fired that shot didn't need to fire again. The yearling would never get up. Well, perhaps it's best if I don't subject you to the crude outburst with which I saluted two of those hunters. It's enough to say I was livid. They took it all too; which proved they knew themselves to be in the wrong. Their feeble excuse was that they had seen the deer from a single high point, the clearing being just visible.

'But you must have known it was in my area,' I burst out.

'Couldn't resist it,' I was told.

Maybe ten years earlier I wouldn't have been as worked up over the experience. But today's scene is completely different. Though that shot wasn't aimed at me, it was still far too close. It was even more shocking because just a few days before a hunter had been carried out of the bush near Puketitiri. He was dead from a shot aimed at a deer.

It's been apparent that since the price of venison dropped, there have been fewer deaths in the field from hunting accidents. This proves that there is less hunting activity. I don't believe hunters are taking more care, as has been suggested. Now that a big cheque doesn't go with a successful hunt, I think many men aren't finding the sheer thrill of hunting for the sake of hunting and winning a trophy is enough. When the price for venison was around the dollar a pound mark, an average of one man a week was being shot in mistake for a deer.

Generally, the guy who cops it is in his early thirties, married and the father of several kids.

To generalise, the one who fires the shot is usually a young man, late teens, early twenties, without much hunting experience. He's apt to become incredibly excited at the sight of a deer and blast off at a noise or a sudden movement without really thinking. He's very bad news in any hunting party.

To be fair, it must be admitted that many a seasoned hunter makes mistakes. The chief cause of trouble in deer hunting is often that it excites a man to a state resembling intoxication. He'll take chances with his personal safety when hunting that normally he wouldn't dream of doing. Above all, he's just bustin' to get his sights on a deer, to send a soft-point bullet on its errand of death. Sometimes he does just that — with deplorable results! Indeed, some men, the quietest of types in town, are suddenly transformed in the hills. Many act like God Almighty when they have a rifle in their hands. Perhaps because they're getting back to something very basic — hunting.

In the majority of hunting fatalities improper identification of the target is the cause. Above all, one must be absolutely certain that it is a deer in the sights. It's no good firing at an indistinct blob in a poor light, or beyond a shaking branch hoping it's a deer.

It has to be a deer!
With hair on!
One that's alive and not draped over some staggering meat hunter's bent back. A good percentages of hunters shot and killed in the past few years have been packing out a deer carcass at the time. One man was shot while packing out a pig!

A sudden flash of reddish-brown in the scrub or bush is all it needs for some fellows to shoot. Pausing and being absolutely sure doesn't come into the matter. Everyone's thought must be, 'Are you sure it's a deer? Could it possibly be a man packing out a carcass, or even a back leg slung over his shoulder?' Whatever the circumstances you'd better put a lot of thought into that quick shot, for it might well be the most important thought you've ever had. And the most important shot you've ever fired.

A top-class scope is a marvellous aid towards determining exactly what you're aiming at. In the deceptive light of early morning and late evening it couldn't be more apparent. I recall sneaking around a large hillface one evening. The light was bad, a fading greyness. Yet a fine time to latch on to a deer. Quite suddenly I spotted two dark and indistinct shapes directly ahead. Aha, I thought with satisfaction. Two deer! It was an obvious conclusion. I'd tailed two deer in almost the same spot a couple of evenings before. The 4x scope was to my eye as fast as I could get it there and those two blurred shapes resolved themselves into two men, crouching down and looking at me. I yelled out loudly; something told me to do so.

It turned out they were glassing me as well, but their scopes weren't top-class and hadn't sufficient light-gathering power for the poor conditions. This was station country and

The Firearms Safety Code

1 Treat every firearm as loaded

2 Always point firearms in a safe direction

3 Load a firearm only when ready to fire

4 Identify your target beyond all doubt

5 Check your firing zone

6 Store firearms and ammunition safely

7 Avoid alcohol or drugs when handling firearms

Further information is available in the ARMS CODE, go to www.police.govt.nz or www.mountainsafety.org.nz

New Zealand POLICE
Nga Pirihimana O Aotearoa
www.police.govt.nz

OUTDOOR SAFETY
NEW ZEALAND MOUNTAIN
SAFETY COUNCIL

New Zealand Government

Seven points you've got to know.

I could have been a sheep, a cattle beast on the small size, a deer. So it was proved when one of the hunters admitted in a shaky voice, 'Jesus! We had you picked for a deer, mate!' It wasn't a cold evening, being early in the year, but I'm telling you I broke out in a cold, cold sweat.

How about the time a hunter was out alone in the country a way back of the Kaweka Range and over towards the Kaimanawas. He was right out in the open tussock when a bullet ripped by him so close that he knew someone had made the classic mistake. There was only one thing to do and he did it — dived headlong into the tall grass.

He was badly shaken up. That shot could easily have nailed him. But he certainly wasn't about to get up and argue the point right then. Instead, he decided he would lie right where he was and teach the useless bastard who had fired at him a lesson he would never forget.

A flushed-with-success hunter came bounding up, peering into the grass for his kill. He had almost reached the spot when his deer leaped up and snarled, 'You … idiot!'

I was told the fellow turned pure white before twisting around and bolting away.

I have always favoured wearing old gear which blends in with the country, but maybe this will have to change. Maybe something along the lines of what they wear in North America will one day be required by law. If you were to meet a hunter wearing a red woollen hat, jacket and pants you'd probably think he was Father Christmas — without reindeer. Still, a case of mistaken identity is a whole lot better than being dead.

During my last year working for a rabbit board in Hawke's Bay, my wife became more and more agitated every time I went hunting, which was understandable. So she came up with a brainwave and machined bright-red strips of material on to my green hunting shirts. I must admit I felt a bright bastard every time I went out wearing them, but the idea did make sense. And one day I met a hunter who said, 'No one would take a crack at you wearing that shirt — those red bits were the first things I noticed.' After that I didn't feel quite so idiotic.

By far the most dangerous time to hunt in this country is in the 'roar', especially during the four-day Easter 'break'. The red stag's roar is generally at its peak then. It's certain someone will be shot. Often more than one man. Many hunters cannot resist their yearly 'roar' trip; it's a time when a man can lure a roaring stag simply by imitating one. Such was the case a few years back when two hunters, both roaring madly at each other, decided to sneak in and get themselves a stag.

The one who shot first is still alive.

I must admit I have never heard a man roaring who didn't sound false. There's something primitive and guttural missing from a man's imitations. To a newcomer to hunting it can sound like the real thing — he must be wary in his reactions if it is not to be a death-trap for humans.

There is no hunter who, having spent a long time at the game, hasn't done something stupid with a rifle in his hands. Anyone who says he hasn't possesses either too much pride to admit it, or a conveniently poor memory. Or maybe he's a white-garbed saint. And I can't recall seeing many of those floating around of late.

I have made errors at times and a couple of them I'm ashamed of. It was fortunate for me, and perhaps someone else, that they turned out as they did. However, in recent years I've been caution itself on the hills and, because of it, have even lost game. Still, isn't that better than being guilty of the biggest mistake a hunter can make?

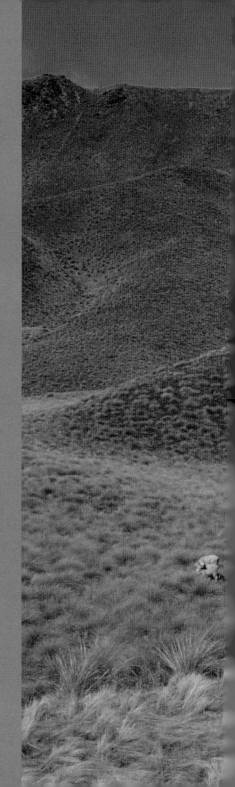

The Deer Hunters — 1976

Where Danger Lurks

Morven Hills — where red deer were first liberated in 1871.

Unlike so many parts of the world, New Zealand has no poisonous reptiles or insects. You may spread a groundsheet and sleeping bag practically anywhere and be entirely safe. Yet, from many causes numerous hunters, climbers and trampers have met their death in the back country — a lonely place to die.

Mainly the tragedies are the result of highly unpredictable weather, allied with the terrain, a person's extremely bad luck, or simply unpreparedness. Unfortunately, accidents and deaths are increasing in the hills. Some mountain safety committees, combined with deerstalking clubs, hold yearly courses in basic bushcraft. The foremost single message they strive to get across is that a person should have some prior knowledge of an area before setting foot in it. There's no excuse for anyone setting out 'blind' and just hoping for the best. One can buy a low-cost Lands and Survey topographical map covering the area to be visited. Then, it might be possible to talk with someone who knows the area well, say a Forest Service ranger or field officer if it's State forest, a National Parks ranger if it isn't. The chances are it will be one or the other.

These men can give priceless life-saving tips, such as where to ford a river should it be in flood, or where a certain wire-bridge is located if the flow of water is too great to cross in a conventional manner. It also pays to check where huts are located, for many a hut is marked wrongly on maps. The numerous deerstalking, mountain safety and tramping clubs around the country are easy to approach. The advice their members give is sound and based on the very best knowledge of all — practical experience.

In remote areas conditions are always tough: bluffy faces, heavy bush where it's so easy to become confused and then lost; tricky rivers and side creeks. Since most back country is also high country, the weather must always be taken into consideration. It's of little use, most of us have found, to believe what we hear when the well-spoken weather forecasts predict, with the utmost confidence, a 'high' covering the entire area. So often this doesn't apply to mountain country. I have watched it snow heavily from a high hut when, according to the forecast, the sun should have been streaming down.

This means that one must be equipped with adequate gear at all times. Many who haven't followed this most basic of rules are past worrying about it now. Most have been victims of exposure, the biggest single killer in New Zealand's back country.

The most hazardous obstacles are rivers and side-streams which can rise in level at an alarming rate, almost unbelievable unless you've actually seen it happen. The wisest advice concerning flooded waterways is to stay put if they look at all risky to cross, even if it means spending a night in the open. You'll be miserable, but that's a long way ahead of being found well downstream with a bloated body and barely recognisable features. Spending a night out isn't too bad if you're not short of the essentials; and rivers in flood generally drop very quickly, often overnight. It is sometimes difficult to recognise the quiet river of first light as that roaring, mud-stained giant of the night before which had the power to uproot trees.

Uncertain footing is another hazard to watch for. Much hunting country is of a crumbling nature and one's footing therefore is unsteady at times. A twisted ankle is no joy in town — it's something else entirely where a man is just an insignificant speck in an immensity of wilderness. Watch for falling rocks in steep places. Remember that a single shot can cause a rock slide, especially in thar and chamois country. Hunters have been known to be underneath when that's happened. It pays to be aware of danger all the time, to be on the alert. Many wild animals are killed when they are relaxed and unsuspecting. There's a lesson in that for man.

The wind can be a treacherous enemy too … I recall Allan Hill and myself backpacking into Pohangina Saddle hut in the early summer of '63 (a miserable, smoky camp high in the central Ruahines). It was so windy we were unable to speak to each other. Not that a man has much to say at such times — he's mainly intent on getting one boot in front of the other.

Allan, a big man who hit the scales around fourteen stone in the raw, was as powerful as a bull, and the frame pack he carried was no load for a weakling. There we were, just topping Stag Spur, and the hut was no distance away. Allan was up front and therefore the first to face a truly ferocious blast from the south. It had the outright and frightening power to lift him and his pack about a foot off the ground. There he hung, suspended as though attached to invisible strings, before being dumped solidly to the ground. It could be said that we were fortunate not to be in really dangerous terrain at the time.

Mist. It's a very nasty hazard all over the country. Often it creeps in from the coast in a downright sneaky fashion, completely blotting out familiar landmarks. It makes steep hill faces seem easier to negotiate than they really are and so deadens sound that one might well be in another world entirely. Deception itself is the swirling mist of the high country.

KNOW BEFORE YOU GO

The Outdoor Safety

CODE

Before you go into the outdoors get familiar with New Zealand's Outdoor Safety Code.

5 simple rules
to help you stay safe:

(1) **Plan your trip**
Seek local knowledge and plan the route you will take and the amount of time you can reasonably expect it to take.

(2) **Tell someone**
Tell someone your plans and leave a date for when to raise the alarm if you haven't returned.

(3) **Be aware of the weather**
New Zealand's weather can be highly unpredictable. Check the forecast and expect weather changes.

(4) **Know your limits**
Challenge yourself within your physical limits and experience.

(5) **Take sufficient supplies**
Make sure you have enough food, equipment, clothing and emergency rations for the worst-case scenario. Take an appropriate means of communication.

Also available:

The Boating Safety
CODE

The Water Safety
CODE

For more information about how you can prepare for your outdoor activity,
visit **www.adventuresmart.org.nz**

Sound advice.

Should you happen to be caught out in misty conditions and quite suddenly feel unsure where you are exactly, the best advice is to stop, sit down and don your thinking cap. Smoke, if you do. Above all, don't blunder on like a blind man without his white stick. And equally important, try to avoid panic. Panic saps strength and energy all too quickly, and one will need all the resistance it's possible to summon. Panic, in itself, is a killer.

On occasions I've been able to get below the level of the mist. Then it has been a simple matter to work out where I was. Mostly though, you're well and truly stuck with the mist, and might end up spending a night out. Once more the message should be driven home: you must have ample warm clothing, matches, a first-aid kit, and some experts suggest a little food wouldn't go amiss either. They're right, too, for there's something comforting about food.

If you are in a position where it's necessary to spend a night out, try to find a dry spot, if it is possible, and light a fire. A fire is always fine company and helps revive flagging spirits. Better still, it'll help to defeat exposure.

I suppose it will be thought by some people that I have laid on the dramatics too much in writing of these natural hazards. But if that is so, then I would ask those folk to consider that in 1973, for example, fifty-six people perished in the hills and in the rivers. Consider that police patrols and civilian searchers rescued another six hundred-odd from trouble of one kind or another in bush and on mountains. In the last six months of the same year, search and rescue teams were engaged on more than three hundred operations, more than half of them in mountain country. Lastly, many of the men killed in that year were experienced, and some of them were deer hunters.

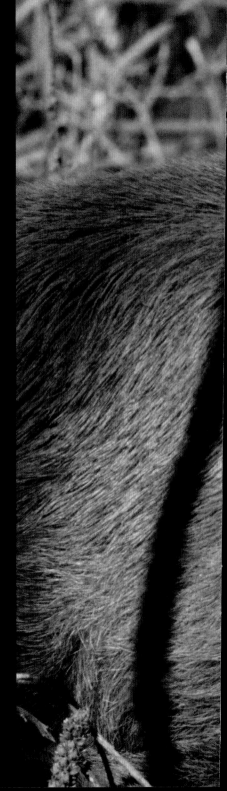

Seasons of a Hunter — 1977

Wild Pigs — Fast Action

This is a fine example of a New Zealand wild boar, displaying the physical characteristics of the European wild boar. He stands about a metre at shoulder height and, at an educated guess, would weigh in excess of 120 kg.

It was a fine but gusty day in the late April of '74. I reached by midday a narrow firebreak that slashed apart a veritable wilderness of thick, jungle-like scrub, close to Burns Range, and south of the Napier to Taihape inland route. It was here that I came across deeply etched and large tracks. They were fresh too, as was the rooting. In fact, you'd have thought a miniature bulldozer had been in action. Or at least one big boar.

In the eighteen or so months that I'd hunted this area, often camping out overnight because it was quite a walk in from the road, and, more importantly, because it put me where I wanted to be at the right time, I had never seen a big boar. On the other hand, I had never once failed to see a deer and had only failed twice to carry out a kill. An ace spot and no mistake.

The deer, red and sika, but mostly red, lived for the most part in Forest Service land. As is often the way they crossed the unmarked border and fed where the tucker was good. On the farmlands, in other words. So who did they really belong to? The Forest Service or Joe Cocky? *Yours*, man! *If* you could nail one good and hard.

But the pig tracks I had seen were uppermost in my mind. Before I ventured off into the bush country I'd check out that firebreak again. It had recently been overturned and ploughed, the soil rich, dark and moist. Irresistible for any member of the porker family.

All that afternoon that pig occupied my thoughts, even though it was deer I was after. A boar! With a mouthful of tusks, razor-edged and of trophy size. Too much time had elapsed since I'd had one of them big 'uns in my sights.

I was still thinking about this boar when a red deer hind leapt up from a belt of high crown fern. She had been unsure; possibly she had just heard a slight noise and had not been fortunate enough to sense me.

I packed the carcass out of the forest, across a stretch of farmlands, still musing over the big boar.

It was early evening when I neared the firebreak. Glad to be rid of the weight, I dumped the carcass down in ferns where it was well hidden. A light breeze fanned my cheeks as it loomed up through a gap in the thinning scrub belt. There was also a suggestion of rain in the air. A good time, then, for pigs to be on the move. Cautiously, I peered over the firebreak. No pigs in sight.

Pushing the last of the scrub to one side, I saw something that caused my insides to tighten up. One of my own recent bootprints was now partly obliterated by a pig's tracks! Just a small one, but it indicated pork on the hoof and where there's one pig …

Checking the time, I found I had about two hours of shootable light left. Which also happened to be about the same length of time it would take me to get out to my Viva, parked along a winding track close to the road. Two hours. A lousy walk with a long hard climb at the end.

It would be best to leave now. And yet this kind of overcast evening definitely suited pigs. If I stayed, then I just might take a trophy home. I mulled this over for about ten minutes, finally deciding to stay.

I started off along the firebreak, heading in an easterly direction and well away from the place of sign. About half a mile further on the firebreak ended at the base of a hill; a big grassy area where I'd dropped a few deer. Not this evening, though; being late April there was little fresh grass or clover to lure them out.

There was about one hour of daylight left; the rain was holding off. Good.

Horses in the Ureweras.

A group of disturbed hinds heading for the safety of the trees.

The country I overlooked was that of a sheep and cattle farm, almost entirely surrounded by the Forestry land, part of which was a huge gorge in which flowed the Ngaruroro River.

In recent times, long after the venison boom, big herds of deer have come out of this gorge and from the heavy scrub below and upon the Burns Range to feed on the farmlands. As many as forty had been sighted. Little wonder, then, that it had known more than its share of cunning poachers, some riding horses and using packhorses to carry out the meat. That's what I should have had at Mangaweka, a good packhorse.

Time started to slip away and I chuckled as an amusing incident came to mind. It had happened just a few weeks back, very close to the Burns Range. At the time I was dressing out a hind. It was getting late, too late if I expected to get to my camp before dark. There I was bending over and making fast actions with my knife, when the stillness of the late evening was rudely shattered by a shrill bleating sound — a goat. Pausing, I glanced around — nothing. No matter; I'd seen enough goats in Hawke's Bay to last a couple of lifetimes.

A few seconds later the out-of-sight goat bleated again. I stopped to quickly look around and, again, nothing. Strange, for I could see quite a distance in all directions. The many deer that had roamed these areas had left little else but odd clumps of fern here and there.

Sheathing the knife, I got the carcass on to my back and then started up a steep, slippery slope of bare earth. On the ridge-top, and glad to be there, I heard the goat again. For the life of me I just couldn't pinpoint the damn thing. So off I set, heading down towards my campsite only forty minutes away.

I'd tramped but a short distance when again there was a bleat. This time right on top of me! Yes, that goat was up a tree! A black-and-white billy about twelve feet off the ground and delicately poised on a none too thick bough. I had to smile, not because it was the first goat I had ever seen up a tree, but because of the shocked expression flooding its face.

Then well down the same ridge others scattered with sharp, carrying sounds so typical of wild goats. Tree-climbing billy was caught in two minds. He wanted to chase after them but, as I was right below him, he was obviously, and understandably, reluctant to do so.

Still smiling, I moved away. That quickly made up his mind. With two sure-footed leaps which took him cleanly from that bough to another and then to the ground, that wild goat ably demonstrated the truly wonderful agility of his breed …

It was starting to get a little dark now; almost time to move. If pigs were going to show themselves on the firebreak before dark, well they'd had time aplenty to do so. Still … a few more minutes wouldn't hurt, it could in fact make all the difference.

I raised my field glasses once more.

Dark blobs, far away. Even so, I knew exactly what they were. Deer, and more deer. They come up from the gorge, if not to feed then perhaps because they were tired of the heavily forested country. They were now scattered over a grassy patch, surrounded by scrub.

I knew that spot. I had been there more than a year back at velvet time when I had come across five big stags feeding where the grass fingered into the scrub. Big stags. With big velvet. A fantastic sight when, at that time, velvet was worth $10 a pound … And then it was time for me to move, to again check out the firebreak. This time I was to be in luck.

Pigs! Five or six of them of average size, heads down, jawing up the blackish, root-filled earth in obvious ecstasy; tails constantly flicking.

Slowly, I moved in on them. The wind was right; light not quite poor. Great! My eyes searched for a big one. Then, from just ahead and inside the scrub cover, I heard the distinct sound of a big pig. The heavy swishing sound that a really large one makes as his great weight pushes aside thick growth.

Ready to shoot, I held my breath …

Suddenly, as though a switch had been turned off, all noise ceased. The silence in comparison was stunning … they were on to me! Then all hell broke loose. Pigs were running in all directions.

One of the bigger pigs raced along like some sort of low battering ram. I whipped Sako to my shoulder. Too late, gone but for the noise. And then, around forty paces from me, a huge boar lunged into sight, whirling within his own body length to face the unwelcome intruder. His expression was one of pure and total belligerence, his anger monumental. Had fire been pouring from his gaping jaws he would have made an effective dragon.

It was time to fire.

The shot hit the boar in the brisket; a solid thump as the soft-point projectile smashed into heavy muscle and bone — infinitely satisfying.

I reloaded, and then quickly moved in, ready to shoot again if need be. But he was dead.

Tusks?

Yes! I now had a pair of sharp-pointed weapons to rank with those I took from the Urewera country in 1966.

The Hunting Breed — 1979

One of the Best

Lake Pearson, Canterbury.

*A deer culler in the late 1940s backpacking his gear and a huge
load of dried deer skins at Totara Point, on the Rakaia River.*

T

he night air was cold enough to penetrate a
thick woollen shirt. Stars glittered like countless
jewels spread upon some endless velvet carpet; the
brilliant moonlight distinctly outlined the long, undulating
hump of the high tops, and cast itself like an enormous
phosphorescent beam over the frosty river-flats. From the
nearby river came a deep but subdued murmur. A night bird
cried out rather forlornly, it seemed, from the heavy beech
forest somewhere behind the Ahaura base-camp hut.

Although I was a stranger in this setting, I nevertheless
felt at peace with my wilderness surroundings. And it
occurred to me then, as indeed it had several times during
my Westland interlude, that I'd really been away from the
hills for far too long a time. Suddenly the cold got to me. I
spun on my heel and started to the hut where I would rejoin
John and Brian …

Like the more famous Karangarua River to the south, the
Ahaura River is in Westland, too. By any standards it is a big
waterway, consisting of several large rivers rising high on
the Main Divide of the Southern Alps. The Ahaura Valley, in
comparison to many others, is an easy one to travel on foot;
there are many long grassy flats and, at regular intervals,
good Forest Service huts to camp in. The open tops appear
more rolling than you'd expect of the region, the bush
slopes are more sloping than sheer. Together they lack
the hostile appearance of much of the West Coast's long
mountain chain. To a North Island hunter such as I there is
a more attractive look to the landscape. It is as though we
could cope here, and well.

The Ahaura Valley also happens to be one of John
Henham's favourite places. In a lifetime largely devoted
to outdoor pursuits, he has possibly spent more time there

than anywhere else. He was talking to Brian and me about the valley, but more about his very colourful past, while we warmed ourselves in front of a cheery log fire in the Ahaura hut …

John Henham of the delicious dry wit is a West Coaster through and through. He was born and grew up in a country area close to the Ahaura Valley. He can't remember a time when he wasn't keen on rifles and hunting. During the days of the Second World War, young Johnny stalked wild goats. They were plentiful, not difficult to hunt. Better still, there was a keen demand for their attractive skins. Average price was about fifteen shillings and because money was a scarce commodity for many in the early 1940s, and also because fifteen shillings was a tidy sum, the keen young hunter shot and skinned as many as he could. It was a good grounding for later years.

Although it may seem strange when you consider how things are today, there was at this time no market for deer. Venison was looked down on; it came from a pest! A deer skin made a fair sort of mat. So now, virtually undisturbed since the war had started, they had multiplied almost beyond belief. They could often be seen grazing on the grassy sides of a country road, even close to towns. And up on the tussocky tops and in the grassy river valleys their numbers were uncountable. It would — said John — take a sudden market for deer skins in the early 1950s to reduce their overall numbers somewhat.

Like many a keen young hunter, John had vivid daydreams about becoming a deer culler. So in 1951 he took the plunge, joining the Internal Affairs Department. They handled the so-called 'Noxious Animals' policy until the Forest Service took over.

Jim Muir, undoubtedly one of the 'great guides'.

Harper River, Canterbury.

John's first block turned out to be the Ahaura. Even though other professionals had worked there, it was still overrun with game. During the late spring and early summer months the river-flats were alive with deer. To secure a good tally, John happily discovered, was simply a matter of sneaking from one quiet mob to the next and opening up with his open-sighted .303. As for chamois they were almost as plentiful as the deer. John was to shoot many on the river-flats, invariably collecting both types of animals in the course of one hunt. Little wonder there is a wistful look about John when he recalls those days that will never return.

As a professional, John was paid the princely sum of five pounds a week. On top of this retainer there was a five shillings bonus for each deer kill, and seven shillings and sixpence for each chamois. Tails only. Deducted from whatever he earned was the Government's slice and thirty shillings for food.

In marked contrast with later years, the food was very basic in those days. Rice was the main commodity — sacks of the stuff. 'A good binder,' the deer cullers said. All supplies had to be backpacked from camp to camp. The way John tells it, this was a real curse, eating into one's valuable hunting time. It would be some years before fixed-wing airdrops would change all that.

As in other parts of the country where the Government's shooting arm was waging total war on the wild ones, roughly made but comfortable tent-camps were the order of the day. The only huts were base camps. Or perhaps the odd station shack where a wandering shooter might stay overnight. Yes, life was undoubtedly tougher in deer-culling circles then. But as John says, a man was young then, lean and fit; there was fantastic hunting to be enjoyed, fish in the rivers, geese on the river-flats. That was the life!

In 1953, after a most successful introduction to professional hunting, John felt a strong urge to see other parts of the South Island. The urge carried him to Canterbury where he worked as a contract shooter — one pound a skin. This turned out to be a far different proposition from mere tail hunting. Huge bundles of dried skins, often weighing as much as 100 pounds, had to be backpacked from various parts of the block to base camps or pick-up points. Contract shooting, John reckoned, wasn't such a good caper. He would return home, having felt the irresistible pull of the West Coast.

Again he hunted the Ahaura block. Sometimes the nearby Haupiri block, too. Then during the miserable wet winters, so common in that part of the country, there were tracks to be cut, linking pathways between camps, making it easier when the next shooting season arrived.

Later on, he came to know other parts of Westland too: the mighty Karangarua for one, and the other valleys, rich in hunting legend, that drain their turbulent waters into it — the Copland, the Regina, the Douglas or, as it's sometimes known, the Twain. Names to make a true hunter's pulse rate soar. Great trophies by today's standards were often shot. Some were taken — most were not. Then sometimes a man would remove the head of a fine stag or thar or chamois and firmly lodge it in the lower branches of a tree, a handy rock crevice — to be picked up later. But as most of the oldtime shooters recall, very few ever were!

John recalls a day in the summer of 1958 in the Karangarua Valley. Still deer culling, he was camped at Christmas Flat hut. Because the day was fine and not too windy, he decided to hunt the tops between the Douglas and Karangarua.

By early afternoon, he was standing on a 5000-foot high point overlooking Cassell's Flat. To his credit, he had the tails of seventy-four chamois and had used up all his ammunition. While returning to camp, he reckoned he could have quite easily shot thirty more of the nimble-hoofed antelope. It's little wonder that he and so many others like him, because of the constant practice, eventually became crack shots on game.

John turned his back on the deer culling a year later. His best day on red deer had been an even fifty. His overall tally, taking all game into consideration, numbered in the thousands. Yet such staggering tallies, as shot by numerous early deer cullers, would in no way threaten the survival of the great game herds of the fabled West Coast. In many places, mostly heavy bush country, the professional shooters weren't even able to keep up with the annual birth rate.

Directly after his deer-culling days, John turned meat-hunter. He and some similarly minded mates shot the thick, deer-infested bush of the Haast Pass country — a bush-shooter's dream come true. They backpacked the carcasses down to the nearest river-flat or level stretch of shingle, practically anywhere that a fixed-winged aircraft could touch down and take off.

The years went by, faster it seemed. By now John was a married man, a father. Yet at no time did he ever stop thinking like the outdoorsman he was. His admirable philosophy regarding his lifestyle was to make his outdoor interests pay for themselves. It had been like that right from the very start, shooting goats for their skins. So there were possums to trap for their valuable winter skins; lucrative whitebait to fish for in season; timber to fell; and, best of all,

Erin Osbourne, on the D'Urville Tops, head of Lake Rotoroa, 1920.

there was profitable deer hunting to be enjoyed whenever the opportunity arose. They were good years.

About the middle sixties someone had an inspired idea which was to drastically change the whole concept of hunting in New Zealand. He reckoned that a helicopter could be used for hunting and recovering the carcasses of deer.

In 1965 John Henham was one of the first men to shoot deer from a helicopter in this country, possibly the very first. The weapon he selected to take aloft with him on that initial flight was a 12-gauge semi-automatic shotgun. He was to soon discover just how limited that was, for while a charge of buckshot was a devastating killer close up, it had no range at all. It also ruined too much meat. Which is why on the third flight the butt of an FN semi-automatic .308 fitted snugly against his shoulder, a steady stream of lead jetting from its muzzle. This was something else. This was murder. His biggest day's tally shooting from the air — one hundred and forty — happened in and around the Arawata Valley.

Some of John's contemporaries are men I have written about before. Napier-based Norm Gilmore, for instance, was one of John's field officers; Jack Wildermoth, my field officer in Southland for a short time, was a fellow deer culler; Keith Purdon another boss.

While talking with Keith Purdon a few months after I returned to the North Island, John's name had slipped quite naturally into the conversation. Curiously, I'd asked him what had John been like as a deer culler. Keith had arched his eyebrows, considered very quickly, and then told me:

'Johnny was one of the best.'

Somehow, I'd reckoned as much.

National Publicity Studios

In the famed hunting ground of the Arawata Valley, Bill Nolan loads another red deer trophy onto his packhorse for the trip out.

On Target — 1981

Chamois

ng towards Mt Cook where chamois were first released in 1907.

I had climbed with haste to above the bush-edge, fighting my way through a tangled, waist-deep belt of tough scrub, up to a world of rimrock, tussock, and tall Spaniard grass. This was the high world of the Southern Alps on a bleak day in late April.

Pausing to catch my ragged breathing, I listened in awe to the sound of red stags roaring out their primeval challenges. There were, I judged, four of them, widely scattered. They'd set up their domains below me in the densely forested country. It was the real reason that I had climbed to an altitude of around 5000 feet; I'd wanted to get well above them, where I would be able to work the wind more to my advantage, always a sound ploy, whatever the game.

In particular it was one stag that I was after — a big, rangy, dark-coated fellow, maybe a ten-pointer. It had eluded me two days before thanks to a hind who'd winded me and barked her disapproval. But now, today, I would be sneaking down, instead of up, to the little herd that had set up camp — the stag's specific territory for the duration of the rutting time — in the fairly open, basin-like head of a steep-sided creek.

Suddenly with a shiver I was aware of how much colder it had become. Moreover, a thick blanket of mist was swirling about the snow-dusted tops a thousand and more feet above me. As I watched, it came spiralling down in silent, engulfing wreaths. As was my habit, I checked out my BSA Hunter .222, used a thick wad of Forestry-issue tissue to dry the moisture-coated lens of the 4x Nickel scope. Slinging the rifle over my Swanndri-clad shoulder I was suddenly aware of being stared at. You know what I mean — a creepy, crawly feeling like clammy fingers probing the base of my spine.

Whirling about, I found myself staring at a chamois near the foot of a rock-studded grass face; a long-legged buck, about forty-odd paces away. He was sporting a thick set of what were obviously trophy-length horns. I did a fast double-take. It was understandable; this just happened to be the very first chamois that I had ever seen in the wild.

Still the buck remained motionless, watching me with prominent eyes that appeared more curious than frightened. Careful to avoid any sudden movements — often so fatal when so close to game — I raised my treble-two with what I now suppose were slightly shaking hands and simultaneously closed the smooth bolt on a 50-grain projectile.

Then, out of the extreme corner of my vision, I foolishly let a sudden movement divert my attention. Yet another chamois, with the same misty backdrop as the buck, pranced rather than walked into view. The newcomer was smaller than the buck, more lightly built, with thinner horns — a doe. Furthermore, her eyes were quickly drawn to mine and I first sensed rather than saw her sudden apprehension.

Then, nearby, a sharp whistle set my teeth on edge. I knew what it was, had read plenty about chamois — a sentry sounding the alarm. Again that same warning whistle pierced the still, cold air — an aged doe, most likely, since they normally qualify for such important roles in chamois circles.

Damn her! I quickly re-aimed at the buck which, in that instant, hunched his fine ropey muscles and exploded (no other word will do) into a whirling, jack-knifing leap. Gone, just like that; lost in the mist. I heard once the sound of his hard-rimmed hoofs striking loose rock. Then nothing; even the stags had stopped roaring. Mist closed in around me so that I was completely engulfed; not a pleasant feeling. The silence of this misty place was deafening. I shook my head in disgust; a chamois buck, a high-scoring trophy more than likely, and so very, very close …

Philip Holden with a chamois buck.
Shot from a range of 250 metres.

Tony Entwistle overlooking the watershed of
the Wairau River, Nelson Lakes district.

Chamois territory. Chamois favour the lower mountain slopes: big grassy basins and sweeping meadows occurring above the bushline at an altitude of around 4500–6000 feet.

But then, most every hunter who has tried his luck after those elusive, high-country dwellers has such a hard-luck story to tell; it's all a part and parcel of stalking what is perhaps the prettiest of all the game animals in this country.

The chamois is found in the mountains of southern Europe through to the highlands of south-east Europe and south-west Asia. Although once shot commercially for 'shammy' leathers (now produced from domestic sheep and goats), they are now almost solely hunted as a trophy animal. As such they are held in high esteem. In Europe, the licence to hunt them costs a great deal, taking the sport of chamois hunting out of reach of the common man. It is a dangerous sport. In fact, more hunters in Europe have been killed in pursuit of this goat-like antelope than any other wild animal.

Chamois were introduced into New Zealand in 1907 when two males and six females (a gift from Emperor Franz Josef of Austria) were liberated on the slopes of Mt Wakefield, near Mt Cook, in the South Island. Here they found mountainous terrain comparable with those countries of which they were native.

By the following year it was noted that some of the does had kids at foot. By 1919 there was a herd of about seventy animals living close to the liberation point. As their numbers steadily increased in a predator-free land where there was also an abundance of feed, so did they spread further afield.

Chamois were carefully protected until 1930 when, as with red deer, high-country runholders complained bitterly that they were competing for feed with their flocks. In 1936 the wildlife section of the Internal Affairs Department, in the form of cullers, took drastic action to reduce their numbers. At no point since then has the chamois, one of the world's most sought-after trophies, been granted any form of protection.

Today the chamois is continually spreading its range. They are well established in an area extending some 220 miles north of the liberation point to some 120 miles south of it. An interesting fact about them is that they have spread further and faster from their liberation point than any other game animal in the country.

Left: Kea — the world's only alpine parrot.

Above: Tony Entwistle uses a 15x spotting scope, essential for spotting and judging trophy chamois at long range.

The Wild Pig in New Zealand — 1982

Those Were the Days

E ven though wild pigs are still plentiful in certain parts of the country, it is difficult today for many of us to envisage just how many of them there once were. But on a rain-lashed December morning recently, not far south of Raetihi, the past was unexpectedly brought to life for me.

It's mostly farming country around there. The steep hills are vividly green, dotted with sheep, and deep fern flourishes in rain-scoured gullies.

In a high-fenced paddock that ran parallel with the road I observed several types of wild game, mostly fallow deer. But it was the sight of a brownish-coloured boar that caused me to stop. He had all the obvious characteristics of a wild one.

Thankful that the rain had stopped I went to the fence. The fallow, resting, ignored me completely, but a big nanny goat trotted towards me with an expectant look on her long, bony face. With no handouts in the offering she pulled a disgusted face and turned away. It was then that the boar ambled over. Of medium size he gave me the distinct impression that if anyone ruled this paddock then it was him. Arrogantly he thrust his hard snout against the wire, sniffing. Had he been caught in the wild? I was aware now of men's voices in the background, loud, commanding voices. Dogs started barking, too. Cattle complained with aggravated bellows. Perhaps I could learn something about the boar that would be to my advantage? As I started towards a stout-railed cattleyard a stockwhip cracked like a .22 calibre rifle.

Three horsemen were in the yard, working cattle with skill. One of them, wearing a wide-brimmed hat and a thick wool shirt, was giving the orders. While no longer young or even

A farmer scans typical wild pig country.

middle-aged — I judged him about seventy — he still looked more than capable of putting in a full day's work. One of the old school.

For several minutes I stood there unnoticed. It didn't matter; I was enjoying seeing what was going on. Then, spotting me, the boss turned his chestnut's head and rode over. A wooden-handled stockwhip was slung over one shoulder. A limply fashioned cigarette drooped from one corner of his generous mouth. Mud-coated spurs were attached to rubber boots.

We exchanged friendly greetings, said that there had been far too much rain of late, and then I asked him about the boar.

'Yeah,' he said, eager to talk, 'he did come from around here. His name's Swanee.'

'Like in river?'

He smiled as he nodded and went on, 'We caught him as a young one. You can't trust him, though. He still thinks he's a wild pig.'

'Many around?' I asked him.

He arched his eyebrows. 'Pigs, y'mean? No, not any more. Too much of the land around here has been broken in, you see. They haven't got the same sort of cover as they used to have.' A deeply reflective expression came to his heavily seamed features. 'But it was a much different story years ago, my word yes! Why, there were more pigs around here than you could shake a flamin' stick at. We had to get out an' hunt them or go under. Simple as that!'

Sensing a story here I told him that I was working on a book about wild pigs and that I'd deeply appreciate hearing about how it had been then.

'A writer, eh? Tell you what, we'll be havin' smoko pretty soon. If you don't mind waiting until we get these cattle in that paddock over there then I'll be only too pleased to help out in any way I can. Suppose you could stand a brew, too?'

Presently, I went with the boss and a youngish shepherd called Bruce Stone to the old homestead. There I had morning tea with the boss's wife and daughter. After that the ladies drove off for a day in Wanganui and with Bruce having returned to work, I listened with enormous interest to a man, who had obviously loved pighunting, relive a time long past.

Dick Coleman, for that was his name, grew up here on the sheep property called Te Paenga. Back in the 1920s much of the land was still unbroken, heavily bushed or thick with scrub, a perfect haven for countless numbers of wild pigs.

Dick's father, Bill, a keen hunter himself, encouraged his son in all aspects of hunting, although young Dick hadn't really needed any prompting. Hunting was life, and that to a spirited youngster began in the surrounding hills, in the scrublands and in the big native forest a way out back. The opportunities to hunt red deer, big-horned goats and mostly pigs were endless.

In the late evening, for instance, and particularly after rain, it was commonplace to see from the homestead as many as thirty to forty pigs out feeding on a big grassy hillface. A friend of the family, Arthur Duncan, once shot sixty pigs in a single paddock. And should a shot be fired in the back paddocks, pigs would appear as though by magic, multi-coloured mobs of them streaming to the nearest cover, a veritable plague of pork.

When Dick left school it was natural that he should work for his father. Dad paid him ten shillings a week and of course his keep. Dick added greatly to this by hunting pigs on the properties of other farmers in the district who

Lloyd Robinson's '63 Winchester propped against one of the biggest boars he ever shot in the Whangamomona district, 1940s.

had a serious problem on their hands. Pigs abounded by the hundreds, or more probably the thousands. For every pig that Dick killed — its snout was his token or proof of a kill — he was paid one shilling by the farmer whose land he had killed it on. A good weekend for Dick and his dogs (he didn't use a rifle then) could result in as many as fifty pigs being caught.

At that point Dick paused in his story. He told me to help myself to more tea and left me to my thoughts. When he came back, he was clutching an old photograph album. 'Might interest you,' he said.

The photographs were mostly faded black-and-whites, the old 120 negative size. There were pictures of the homestead not long after it had been built. It was considerably smaller then and the people posing before it were dressed like pioneers. But the pictures I saw were mostly of hunting. (No one frowned on hunting then; the wonderful *Weekly News* magazine often published articles and pictures relating to hunting, and pighunting material was particularly welcomed by the magazine's editorial staff.) There were shots of trophy stags and of big boars and panting dogs and horses standing quietly in the background. Somehow they filled me with a deep nostalgia. They were of a New Zealand long since past.

One picture, that of an especially large boar, brought a natural question to mind: 'Suppose you've had a few dogs ripped, Dick?'

He laughed with an icy humour at that. 'Yeah … you could say that.'

Like so many pighunters in this country, Dick has lost his share of pig dogs. They were good dogs as a rule, of mixed breeds, dogs with brave hearts and boundless courage, willing to die for their masters.

And Dick himself hadn't gone without injury. Once when attempting to stick a boar he had been ripped in the forearm — a deep, painful gash that required six or seven stitches; he couldn't remember exactly. Then, later, a boar slashed open his groin. Dick indicated with his finger just where he meant, high on his inner thigh. 'Needed sixteen stitches that time,' he said, shaking his head so ruefully that it might have only recently happened. 'Hell, I came too bloody close to losing you know what that time!'

But that didn't put him off hunting pigs. A real pighunter is exactly the same as a real pig dog in that the pursuit of pigs is a lifelong thing, a consuming passion. Many men participate in the sport until they can no longer climb a hill or swing a leg over the back of a horse. One of Dick's contemporaries was an outstanding example of that.

Russell McLean was his name and he owned a small farm not far from Dick's place. Like many of the men in the district he was an avid pighunter. Hunting pigs was really his life, but his pighunting activities were brought to a sudden end by the Second World War. While overseas, he was unlucky enough to lose a leg. But that on his return to New Zealand didn't stop him from hunting. Fitted out with a wooden leg and mounted on a good horse, he was often back into the fray and packed out as many pigs as he had before the war.

'Yeah, he was a hard old devil, that Russ,' chuckled Dick reflectively, shaking his head with admiration for the man. 'He lives in Tauranga now, I hear.' He paused. 'Of course there were any amount of pigs for him to get out after. They'd bred up like you wouldn't believe during the war years — just like deer and all the other wild game did … most of the hunters were called up, you see.'

It was a bitterly cold day in the late winter of 1940 when Dick, with good reason, vowed that he would never again hunt pigs without a rifle to fall back on. At the time they were again having serious troubles with lambkilling pigs, losing newly born lambs at a terrifying rate. Something had to be done about it.

Just after daybreak on this particular day, on a frost-crusted flat near the Mangawhero River, Dick and his dogs came across what were almost certainly the villains: five highly dangerous-looking boars dominating a fair-sized mob. The boars were all black, sinister somehow, and it crossed Dick's racing mind that it must be extremely rare to see so many large and obviously evil-intentioned boars together. They made no attempt to run. Suddenly to Dick, his dogs and his curved-bladed hunting knife at his belt seemed totally inadequate for the situation.

The dogs, a good team, went in fast. The boars quickly formed a defensive semi-circle around the rest of the pigs and fought like Gurkha troops, savagely efficient.

With stomach-churning horror a helpless Dick watched as three of his dogs went down screaming, bleeding from deep wounds. They died there. Only then did the pigs break. After that chilling encounter Dick made sure that a .303 rifle was slung over his shoulder when he went out after pigs, its ten-shot magazine crammed with solid-nosed military ammunition.

Yet another boar, a gigantic black-and-white one, was to cause Dick many sleepless nights before he finally caught up with it one bleak dawn. Close to where the boar was resting, under a hollow log, were scattered the remains of eighteen lambs; their skins, attached to head and hocks, licked and sucked as clean as a whistle. When confronted by the dogs this boar was too bloated to run, too full to fight back. With a well-aimed head shot, Dick, with grim satisfaction, despatched that particular lambkiller to wherever dead boars go to when they depart from this world.

Dick went on to tell me that it was only when poison was introduced into the area, and its use became widespread, that the huge numbers of pigs were cut back drastically. He frowned then. 'Never had any time for poison, you know. Never once used it on my place. Not once. Can't stand the stuff!' He took a deep breath. 'It killed far too many dogs for one thing.' Dick's expression turned sad and a little wistful. 'Those were the days all right, eh?'

By the time I said goodbye to Dick, mist had gathered about the steep hillface behind the homestead and the grass gleamed wetly. Once, in the late evening and especially after rain, it had been possible from where I now stood to see as many as forty pigs feeding there.

A party of sheep farmers in 1933. In defence of their flocks, they had to relentlessly hunt the wild pig.

The Wild Pig in New Zealand — 1982

A Sow and Her Young

Already using his nose, this little guy is sure to have his mum somewhere close by.

In the winter of 1966 I was hunting professionally in the valley of the Tauranga River in the Urewera country. The valley from a hunter's point of view was a wonderful place, as it was possible to see wild pigs almost every day. Not only did I shoot a lot, but I was also able to observe them closely and to become aware of their habits and their peculiarities.

One warm July afternoon I was up on the sun-splotched slopes above the river where the forest canopy was often low and there was ample food for the hunted ones. About three o'clock I was suddenly faced with a huge windfall, a tangled heap of solid-trunked trees and thinner branches. The largest tree had been uprooted some distance up the bank to my left. Its roots resembled the badly gnarled fingers of a very old man as they clawed above the deep crater-like hole they'd been torn from. The main trunk of this forest giant was massive. Because of the angle at which it had fallen, a section of it, upon a bench, was positioned about two feet off the ground, leaving a gap mostly covered with ferns. I noticed very little of this and simply pressed on angling uphill to avoid the roots.

Suddenly I heard a high grunt, and a large, tan-coloured shape exploded out of the narrow gap under the tree. Right behind it, nearly falling over themselves in frantic haste to keep up, were a many-shaded assortment of piglets. The noise they made was as frantic as it was considerable. The sow, not breaking stride, made a great deal of noise about it too.

Curious about where they'd come from, I slung my rifle and, grabbing a handy branch, hauled myself up and onto the huge trunk directly above the narrow gap. On the other side was a cleared area of two or three yards' circumference, enclosed on one side by the main trunk and on all others by thick-knotted limbs and interlaced branches. Undergrowth and ferns had sprung up in the gaps, so that from ground-level on the outside it would have been impossible to see inside. There was only one way in and out. I lowered myself into what amounted to a suntrap. The pregnant sow had first rooted out the contours of the earth to create a scooped-out hollow. Using her versatile jaws, she had gathered ferns and bracken and bits of grass to line it. The grass had probably come from the banks of a stream about fifty yards away. The lining formed a soft, spring mattress four to six inches thick. The sow obviously believed in comfort, not only for herself but also for the young ones she would soon give birth to.

Where they had been all lying together was warm to the touch, caused by body heat and the sun. I noticed that a few of the sow's crinkly tan hairs were lying upon, or were intermingled with, the well-flattened bedding. Despite a careful check, I found no trace of droppings, nor could I detect a smell of urine.

In captivity, forced by man to live amid muck and garbage, the sow would have been judged by many as a dirty animal that loved to wallow in her own droppings, that relished eating slop another pig might have just urinated upon rather than seeking out her own food supply.

But in the wild, a pig is a far from dirty animal as the sow's nest clearly proved. In this instance, we can only suppose that she had cleaned up any mess her youngsters had made, in the manner of a cat with kittens.

As a rule a sow is ready to breed at around eight to ten months of age. The gestation period is thought to be the same as with domestic pigs, about four months. A sow may have two litters in the course of a single year and, because there is no definite breeding season where a boar is concerned, she may also give birth at any time of the year. Because of warmer weather, when there is a lower mortality rate among newly born pigs, one is more likely to observe a sow with suckers in the spring and early summer.

A sow is equipped with twelve teats. She may give birth to that number of piglets; she may, and very often does in a domestic situation, far exceed it. An exceptional litter could number eighteen; a rare one as many as twenty-four.

In the wild state it is an entirely different story because, for some unknown reason, a sow has a much more modest brood to look after. A likely number to contend with is six to eight. However, these figures are only a generalisation as litters higher and lower in numbers are frequently encountered by hunters.

It was during this same winter, and in a similar location, that I happened to take a break from the day's hunting, which, during the winter, is largely confined to the bush and is therefore tiring. I had my back propped comfortably against a tree, and with the sun streaming down through the forest ceiling it was a pleasant spot to kill a bit of time. Most likely I was daydreaming about things far removed from hunting when a black piglet poked its wee nose out of some nearby undergrowth and then moved warily towards me. Almost at once another tentative head appeared in much the same spot, then, a second or two later, a third little pig revealed itself.

I kept perfectly still, hardly daring to breathe in case she heard my heartbeat, which seemed abnormally loud. Above all, I was curious to see what they got up to.

By now the first little pig had reached the toe of my boot. Sniff, sniff it went and backed away hurriedly. What was the curious thing? Then another moved up to me with jerky, puppet-like movements. It also came close to the toe

Winchester Model 92 Lever Action Saddle Ring Carbine — a favourite rifle for any pighunter.

of the boot, and stared up at me with screwed-up eyes that would never be its strongest feature. Soon there were seven black piglets all around me, investigating everything with the natural curiosity of the very young. Now and then one would become quite bold and would edge right up to me, sniff hard, and then quickly retreat to what it considered a safe distance. One clambered over my legs and gave a prolonged burst of tiny squeals that held, as far as I could tell, no hint of fear. It was a wonderful experience.

In retrospect it was surprising that I saw or heard nothing of their mother. Because they were in such fine condition, they must have had one. Moreover, she would have been close, probably very close. And what, I have since asked myself, would have happened had I picked one up? Certainly the little one would have been distressed and would have shown it with high-pitched cries, sounds that would have carried far in the bush, all the way to the mother's highly tuned ears. A hunter called Rick Knebble did pick up a wild piglet in the bush. This is what happened to him:

At the time Rick, a big, strongly built nineteen-year-old, was also hunting in the Urewera. He was a deer culler who, like so many of them, liked nothing more than to get out after pigs with his dogs. He was in low ponga when his dogs caught a piglet. Knowing that unless he intervened quickly they would kill it, he scooped up the terrified youngster. Naturally it made one hell of a commotion. So did the dogs as they tried to leap up and grab it. Rick lashed out with his boots, then suddenly became aware of a big dark shape rearing up beside him. He'd spotted her too late — the sow already had his calf muscle in a vice-like grip. She shook his leg like a dog with a bone. (A pig is claimed to have the worst bite of any mammal, except for the killer whale, because of the ripping, rather than slicing, motion of its elongated teeth.)

Rick screamed as he tried to shake off the sow; his dogs were stunned. The sow kept on shaking his leg, tearing, ripping. The pain that flared up was like white-hot needles pressing into his brain. In desperation he hurled the piglet into the fern. Unhurt and no longer vocal, it hurried off. It was the best thing he could have done — the sow released her terrible hold and went after her young one. It took forty-six stitches to position Rick's calf muscle back perfectly in place.

Perhaps a young pig's first real impressions of life are those of the warm and satisfying liquid it can drink at length from its mother's teat. It would also be aware of others in the nest: brothers and sisters — squealing, squabbling, food-and-attention-demanding babies. So too would the snugness and the overall security of the nest be something that any young pig would become increasingly aware of.

A nest may well be located in a position similar to the one I described earlier, or it may be positioned under a bank facing the sun or under a raised log or simply in the middle of a clump of thicket-like growth. But wherever it is, the mother will have invariably selected its location with utmost care, a position virtually impossible for man or beast to inadvertently stumble across. Also she will have constructed it well away from her normal haunts, away, in fact, from the pigs she normally lives in close proximity with, choosing a self-inflicted isolation. And with good reason. Pigs, living in small groups, frequently bicker and serious fighting takes place. A boar's temper is notoriously short. A random bite, perhaps given in a burst of adult rage, could easily prove fatal where a little one was concerned.

In choosing exactly where she will give birth, a sow uses her brainpower. Which raises a logical question: how intelligent is a pig? The domestic variety which is confined to a pen or paddock has very little opportunity to

Left: Some things never change when you are chasing pigs — carrying them out of steep gullies, as James Lucas is doing, is one of them.

Causing large-scale damage to good pasture land, pigs can root down a metre or so. Ross Vivian surveys the damage.

reveal its intelligence. To such a pig, life is indeed simple. Everything is laid on: food, shelter, a partner to mate with. The prime object is to produce more bacon. A tame pig's life is therefore suitable only for a very basic creature — a cow, say, bovine of mind, lacking real fighting spirit, fully domesticated, totally dependent on man.

Yet animal psychologists, carrying out extensive tests on pigs, have discovered much to their surprise that they are considerably more intelligent than dogs or cats, and that they rate very close to the great apes in IQ. This would explain why some adult boars are such cunning fellows, possessing the mental capacity to frequently outsmart man and his dogs.

Among the various types of animal feeders there is a group known as omnivores (eaters of everything). Such a sweeping statement is very nearly true in the case of the pig, as it will eat *almost* everything. The ostrich belongs to the same select group. Like the pig, it will eat both plant and animal life more or less indiscriminately.

In Australia, for instance, where wild pigs are similar to those found in New Zealand, they will readily kill and eat venomous snakes. One might suspect from this that they are naturally immune to the effects of the snake bite but this is not the case. They rely for immunity from an otherwise fatal bite on a tough resistant hide, and, just as importantly, on a thickish layer of adipose tissue that directly underlies it. Moreover they possess, like the snake-killing mongoose of

India, faster muscular movements than a snake.

The pig, a most thorough chewer of its food, will consume virtually everything edible it can reach. It will also eat quite willingly the dung of other animals, if the situation warrants it. Like the domestic fowl, it has been observed to eat cow manure. It is able to do so because of a rather unique body, a system, it would seem, that is built for survival in the most harsh circumstances, and allows a pig to find a source of food in what others have passed through their bodies in rejection. Indeed, should a pig be confined to a yard and be fed nothing but a very limited amount of whole grain, it will eat any faeces that contain undigested grain.

A piglet, then, about to leave the nest, is ready to devour absolutely anything it may come across. By following its mother and by taking notice of her example, it will be introduced to a wide and wonderful array of food. Feeding mainly at night, it will consume such bush delicacies as the starch-rich roots of fern and bracken, finger-length and chewy, or such tasty items as worms and fat succulent grubs. A dead deer or an opossum or goat or even a cattle beast might be on the menu. Or perhaps a quick trip, after dark, of course, to a farmer's crop of potatoes or chou moellier. Food is seldom a problem for a wild pig.

Given its omnivorous nature, a young pig has the perfect tools to maintain its food supply. It has teeth like chisels, jaws like a powerful vice, and a snout that is hard and linked by a pre-nasal bone to a very muscular neck and shoulders. The total effect of this combination is a perfectly designed lever that allows a pig to break up hard-packed earth and to shatter by persistence partly rotted logs wherein many grubs can be found.

Each day a young pig learns something new. It will discover that by using its snout it can easily turn over the earth, and that below the surface there is a ready source of food. Even the soil they may inadvertently swallow while in the quest of something tasty is of value to them. In fact, the iron-rich soil is far more important than that — it is absolutely vital to their well-being.

A young pig will subconsciously note that the ground is far easier to work after heavy rain — a more advantageous time to do so, because worms and grubs tend to come much closer to the surface of the ground during and after rain.

Eventually, a young pig puts the nest behind him. He is well prepared for a new way of life. He possesses an exceptional sense of smell and acute hearing, but, it is thought, rather poor eyesight. No matter, for the lack of good eyesight is more than compensated for by a generous helping of sixth sense, that of intuition and perception. This sixth sense, when combined with that uncanny sense of smell, will help him survive. It is just as well that a pig is so well equipped. It is a hazardous life in the wilds of New Zealand.

The Wild Pig in New Zealand — 1982

Lambkiller

*If he gets a taste for lamb, a boar this size
can become real trouble to a farmer.*

In the back country the word 'lambkiller' invariably sums up a rogue boar. So how and why does a boar become a lambkiller in the first place? The most likely explanation is that while foraging for food on pasture lands, it will come across the foetal membranes from lambing ewes. A meal laid on, so to speak. Quickly it eats it up, and finding it to its liking, it hunts with enthusiasm for more of the same. Perhaps it finds it, perhaps not. Its nose, for instance, might lead it to a dead lamb, a real feast. Greedily it devours the carcass. Still not satisfied it continues to search. On this particular night, or the next, a ready source of afterbirth or dead lambs will inevitably run out. The boar will now turn its attention to the newly born lamb, largely incapable of making voluntary movements. The lamb's mother, unfortunately, can offer her helpless young no protection at all.

So it goes on. Once a boar has enjoyed the fruits of lambing time, then the die is firmly cast. Another lambkiller is ready to create yearly havoc with a farmer's livelihood. Moreover, it will uncannily know just when and where to look for them.

The moonlight was unusually powerful as it illuminated a sharply formed hillside in the Waitakere Ranges. Ewes and their lambs moved peacefully about the short-cropped grass. Only the infrequent, unalarmed bleat reached the ears of Arthur Gregory as he sat cross-legged in the closed-in back of his Land Rover. Beside him on an old mattress lay a 12-volt portable spotlight and a much-used Remington .30-06 rifle, Model 743. Looking out over the raised tailboard, he was there for a specific reason, to kill, if possible, a lambkiller.

This story, which took place in the early 1970s, really started a few days earlier when Hap Wheeler had been riding around that same hillside shortly after daybreak. He had been badly distressed at what he had encountered: the bloodied remains of at least five newly born lambs. He decided to enlist the help of Arthur Gregory, who, at this time, was fencing in the district. Arthur, as expected, had been delighted to offer his services.

That night, Arthur with Hap and his son, John, set off to check several paddocks where ewes were expected to give birth. With the wind to their advantage, they slowly worked around two paddocks. Then, in the third, they heard a sudden drumming of hoofs. A pig, indistinct in the pale moonlight, was galloping at breakneck speed along the fenceline. Arthur switched on his spotlight. Magically, the pig — a boar — was cast in a spreading circle of intense light. It started to slow down and wheeled in closer to the fence, ducking towards a small section of partially raised fencing. Arthur fired at that point. While there was no tell-tale thump to indicate a solid hit, he was quietly confident that he'd made a telling shot. But there was no dead pig on the other side of the fence, no blood trail either.

'Reckon you must've missed after all,' Hap said, disappointed.

Arthur ran the tip of his tongue around the roof of his mouth.

'Maybe ...' was all he said.

Still they searched until, suddenly, Arthur noticed a dark hump. It was the boar, dead. Hap was delighted and slapped Arthur on the back, saying that he hoped that this was the end of it. It seemed likely. There was, they discovered, unmistakeable evidence in the boar's bulging stomach to convict it of lambkilling.

After dawn, and in one of the steeper paddocks on the place, Hap was stunned by the sickening sight of more dead lambs; five of them in a small radius. All of which explains why, fifteen hours later, Arthur Gregory was keeping up his patient surveillance of that very same hillside …

Slowly he uncapped a thermos flask of coffee. He drank it appreciatively and thought at length about the boar. One thing was for sure; he could count on the sheep warning him if the boar did return. They reacted to a killer in their midst in exactly the same terrified fashion as they did with a pack of blood-crazed dogs.

It was about 10.30 p.m. and the grass, glittering under the fluorescent-like lighting, was tipped with frost. Feeling the cold, sensing that he might be in for a long wait, he removed his boots and slipped gratefully into his down-filled sleeping bag. That was much better. In that same cross-legged position as before, he raised a pair of bulky 10x50 National field glasses. Methodically he scanned the hillside, which seemed to leap dramatically at him. Because of the strong magnification, sheep and their lambs stood out clearly, appeared so close that he felt all he had to do, to touch one, was to reach out a hand. A magical illusion. Many of the lambs were playing now, chasing each other, such a peaceful scene. It seemed almost impossible that something could suddenly change it, turn the hillside into a place of horror. He wondered how long it would remain like that.

Time dragged by. He was restless. But this waiting game was what outwitting a lambkiller was all about; the only way you could kill some boars. Those ones were as crafty as hell,

John Williamson, with his horse, .30-30 Winchester and a wild boar, typifies the resourceful New Zealand pighunter. Mangapurua Valley.

and had their dens in the most awful places, deep in the bush, often where it was steep, maybe three or four miles from where they regularly killed. Only the very best of dogs could locate them. Even then there was a strong possibility that the boar wouldn't bail, that it would keep on running. And even if they did bail and a dog got hold of it, then they had the strength and the will to break free. It could go on for hours like that. In the end the boar would win out. They were the ones you didn't normally hear about, that never made front page news. The dogs, defeated, shattered mentally and physically, would limp back to their masters who, much to their disgust, hadn't even caught a glimpse of the boar. Often some dogs didn't come back, were never seen again. Yes, thought Arthur, this was the way to play it with the crafty ones, let them come to you.

Arthur's mind started to drift. He remembered that his father, Jack, had shot a lambkiller near this very spot. He thought about some of his own hunts after pigs, some successful, some not. There were no guarantees that you were going to win out with a lambkiller. Many of them were far too smart to ever get caught. They lived to be very old pigs, died of natural causes.

Sheep were bleating with alarm. Arthur stiffened. Taking a deep, steadying breath he reached for his 10x50s. He trained them on the hillside, moving them slowly from left to right. There, hold it! His grip tightened on them. Sheep were jolting downhill, a few, pausing, looked back over hunched shoulders. He followed the line of their sight, saw a big, dark-bodied shape. Sucking in his breath sharply,

Colin Ashmore, a diehard pighunter, on the Pisa Range with his dogs, Winchester .30/30 and a sizeable boar.

he focused his field glasses a shade more precisely and watched avidly as the boar, wheeling back and forth, in the manner of a sheepdog, started to drive the sheep downhill towards the bottom fenceline where the land shelved off and rushes took advantage of the swampy ground.

Quickly he slipped out of his sleeping bag, and felt with chilling impact the frost-tinged air. Shivering, he reached with haste for his boots. Minutes later he was carefully angling down a slippery slope comparable in size to the one he had been observing. About midway down he stopped. No need to rush things. With the tip of his tongue he wet his finger, raised it. What little wind there was seemed to be in his favour. He dropped to his haunches, eager to see what was going on a mere 200 yards away.

The boar was driving everything before it and Arthur knew that what he was witnessing had been seen by few men, the type of thing that some, unaware of how intelligent a pig was, would openly ridicule. But to Arthur, whose respect for boars went back a long way, it only emphasised just how clever some of them were.

Again he tested the wind. It was the same as before. He could approach the other paddock in more or less a direct line. Carefully, he started down.

He was close now, near the fence that separated both paddocks. He had decided to use his spotlight only if it became absolutely essential. His reasons were based on past experiences, for pigs were a most unpredictable animal.

Often he had played a light on a small mob of pigs and they had carried on as though nothing had happened. But put that same light on a boar, one that was 'light-shy', and he'd be head down and off like a shot from a cannon. One thing was certain: pigs hardly ever stared back at a spotlight

in the transfixed fashion that deer and opossums do. Often you could only see one small eye, sunk deep, not nearly as bright as that of a deer. To Arthur they had appeared both green and red. Yes, it was better to avoid using a spotlight if you possibly could. On such a brilliant night as this, and with his 3x9 Kahles scope, he had every confidence in himself to pull it off.

As he moved closer to the fence he was about 100 yards from the boar, certainly no further. Even with the naked eye Arthur could see him quite clearly, motionless in this instant. Arthur put the scope on him, was tempted to shoot. Then the boar moved again, to cut off a darting ewe. At last the sheep were neatly boxed in. The boar rushed them then, went right into the mob. They broke before him and bleating incessantly started to stream up the hill. The boar had failed to grab hold of a lamb. Arthur wasn't surprised. Most, if not all, of the lambs here were nearly a week old. They could run like the wind.

Then the boar was charging uphill, moving fast, incredibly fast, considering how steep it was. With great, lunging bounds it soon drew ahead of the leading sheep. Once past the leaders the boar spun around and started to move from side to side. His intentions were obvious: he was about to perform the same routine. Maybe this time his sudden rush wouldn't prove a futile one.

Kneeling, Arthur pushed his rifle under the bottom wire and then eased his body between the two topmost wires. Gathering up his Remington, he crouched next to a clump of rushes.

Down towards him came the frantic sheep. They were more ordered this time; it was as if they knew what was expected of them. Many of them called out in terror; the harsh, bawling sounds of lambs separated from their mothers. Behind them, big and terrifying, came the killer boar.

Still Arthur waited, watching with narrowed eyes as the sheep started to spill into the rushes. He took a deep breath, slipped off the safety catch. The Remington, with its special eight-shot magazine, was a formidable weapon.

The boar was close to the reeds, slowing, nearly on flat ground. It was close enough, should he wish, to rush at the sheep again. He was now angled to his right, coming closer to where Arthur waited. One moment rushes hid him from view, the next instant they didn't.

He looked ahead of the boar, at a spot between two clumps of rushes and trained his scope on it. He would fire as soon as the boar appeared. Somehow the scope gathered in more light than seemed possible.

Suddenly, he was looking at it, closer than he'd judged. The boar was almost filling the round circle of light. He touched rather than pressed the trigger.

The muzzle flash resembled a sheet of flame from a mythical dragon's throat. The boar, hit low in the shoulder, shuddered under the impact but didn't go down. Nothing probably existed in the boar's mind now but a great roaring fire in his body. Pain, unlike any he had ever known, threatened to consume him. But he was determined to live; that too was a raging fire inside him. So he ran, somehow he ran, towards the hillface, and started up it as Arthur's .30-06 thundered for a second time.

Suddenly the boar's hip was on fire too, could no longer support him. He dropped and lay there — gasping, dying. Then he might have been aware of something looming over him. But his life ended there, ended instantly.

Ejecting the spent cartridge, Arthur turned on his spotlight, flashed the light on the boar's twitching body. He noted its badly ripped ears and good-sized tusks, saw its snarling, blood-flecked mouth, frozen rigid in death. Somehow he knew that Hap Wheeler's troubles were at an end.

As we have noted before, many farmers in this country have been driven to the brink of total despair by the activities of lambkilling pigs. Some have suffered staggering losses. The same thing can still take place today.

The following story took place on a sheep farm in the same valley featured in [another] chapter. The owner, then seventy-two years old, was not in the habit of carrying a rifle. Perhaps because of his age, he wisely shied away from taking unnecessary risks. On this particular winter morning of 1980 he was checking several paddocks where, in the last week, some of his ewes had started lambing.

Before long, his deeply trenched face was set in a bleak scowl. Since he'd been there yesterday morning, a lambkiller had struck and killed at least a dozen times. The pitiful remains, bits of wool and heads and hocks, were all that was left of them.

Checking his mount near a patch of muddy ground, he observed with a knowing eye a single set of tracks. They were deeply imprinted, broad at the toe, those of a boar. He had a hunch that a lone boar was responsible. While he had naturally seen this type of thing many times, he was still filled with the same sense of burning hate and frustration he had experienced in the past. He turned his head and looked bleakly at the nearby forest. Somewhere in there was the boar, safe in his den. He was most likely sleeping off the effects of a too heavy meal.

A home-made and effective pig trap.

Again he turned his attention to the sobering remains of the lambs. He would have to get rid of them soon, burn them or bury them. If he didn't, then other pigs could possibly clean up what was left. They in turn, acquiring the taste, could become lambkillers; a vicious circle.

Worried, he fingered his jaw. Almost certainly the boar would come back tonight, wouldn't be able to resist the temptation. What to do? Then he smiled. Bob Goodall was coming back next day for a few days' hunting. If anyone could get the boar, then it was Bob.

He rode on, slowly, his day already ruined. He wished he could deal with the boar himself. He pulled a wry face; the wrong side of seventy was certainly no age to be mixing with a big and dangerous boar.

Riding into a light breeze, he let his horse pick its own way around a boulder-strewn hillside. Beyond it was a grassy flat, a sure place to find his stock. What he saw there caused him to suddenly stop his horse, and to sit there, stunned. A big ewe in full wool was lying on her right side, bleating in a ghastly fashion as she gave birth. Well, premature birth often occurred; it was a reason why men working a lambing beat sometimes were able to assist with a difficult birth and thus save a life. So it wasn't a ewe giving premature birth that caused the old man's face to flood with revulsion. It was the sight of a big black boar, slowly devouring the membrane-encased lamb as it left its mother's body.

The old man's stomach turned. Then, steeling himself,

TJ with his formidable pack of pig dogs. The rifle is a bolt-action Ruger .223.

his face turned hard, determined. He gathered up the reins. But before impulsive thought was harnessed into positive action, good sense returned to him. What could he possibly gain by chasing off the boar? The lamb was already dead, the ewe, he felt sure, would never get up again. Then there was the boar. It might react violently at being disturbed. Certainly he was mounted on a fast horse. But a boar was quick off the mark too. Some said just as fast as a horse over a short distance. There was always the risk that, should a boar dart between a horse's front and back legs, it could suddenly whip up its head and disembowel it. Yes, it made good sense to keep well out of it.

As he uneasily sat on his horse, he noticed that the boar's feet were ginger right up to its hocks. He couldn't recall ever seeing a pig marked like that before.

The boar, having finished the lamb, now turned its attention to the stricken ewe, dropping its huge head as though about to charge her. The old man tensed, but it didn't come to that. Instead the boar began to turn over the earth about her and, grunting, gradually worked itself into a near frenzy. The ewe struggled wildly to get up. No use. She flopped back, drained, bleating, a cry for help.

Unable to take any more, the old man rode off. Next morning he returned. All that remained of the ewe was a heap of wool. Sighing, he dismounted and untied a long-handled shovel from his saddle.

That morning, Bob Goodall was sipping tea in an old hut he'd camped in before. When he heard the sound of hoofbeats, he went outside to see who was approaching. He greeted the old man warmly and asked him if he had time for a cup of tea.

'Not right now, Bob,' he said. 'But thanks all the same.' He dismounted stiffly and then in a tense fashion he explained what had taken place.

Bob listened to the incredible story, shaking his head from time to time. Then, turning to the hut, he said, 'Last night, eh?' The old man nodded. Bob smiled coldly. 'After eating a whole ewe I doubt very much if he'll go too far.'

'Exactly my sentiments,' the old man agreed.

'I'll get after him right away.'

'Appreciate it, Bob.'

The old man ran the back of his hand across his cheek. 'Thing is, a boar like that could easily cost me half my flock unless he's stopped real quick.'

Bob nodded grimly as he picked up his Sako .222. 'Not to worry,' he said with confidence. 'We'll get him for you.'

'Let's hope so.'

'Ginger feet, you said?'

So Bob and his dogs, Tess and Zapper, set off to locate the boar with ginger feet. As Bob had thought, he hadn't gone too far from the grassy flat and with a dog like Tess on the hunt it wasn't too long before they found him in his ferny bed. Lacking fight, he bailed easily — a simple kill. But despite this, the old man's troubles with lambkilling continued. Later in the year, he sadly told a stunned Bob that he had lost about 60 per cent of his lambs during the season.

Thar

Thar
(*Hemitragus jemlahicus*)
Male: Bull   **Female**: Cow   **Young**: Kid

Range

The thar, often referred to as the Himalayan thar, is a native of northern India. Principally it is found south of the Himalaya, ranging from Kashmir to Bhutan, where it inhabits mountainous country to an altitude of approximately 12,000 feet. It belongs to the sub-family Ovicaprinae of the hollow-horned ungulates. Apart from *Hemitragus jemlahicus*, this select group includes the Arabian thar (*Hemitragus jakaria*) and the Nilgiri thar or wild goat (*Hemitragus hylocrius*). Incidentally tahr is an alternative spelling.

Liberations and Distribution in New Zealand

In his fascinating 1924 publication, *The Game Animals of New Zealand*, T. E. Donne wrote about the introduction of thar into this country: 'In 1904 the Duke of Bedford, in response to a suggestion made by Mr St George Littledale, selected from his herd at Woburn six Himalayan tahr and presented them to the New Zealand Government. It was the intention of His Grace to send eight animals, but two of them escaped from captivity just before they were to be shipped. The six tahr, three of each sex, were forwarded in the SS *Corinthic* which left Plymouth on 6th April, 1904. They were consigned to the Government Tourist Department and reached Wellington in May following. On the voyage they were in the care of the ship's butcher. Each male was put into a separate crate 5x5 feet x 4x6 feet and the three females in two crates. The supply of food for the voyage consisted of twenty bundles of clover hay, carrots, compressed cattle food, and crushed maize. One male got loose and was lost overboard, but the others reached New Zealand in good condition and were quarantined on Some's Island, Wellington Harbour, and afterwards liberated in the Mount Cook district.'

For the record, Mr St George Littledale, an Englishman, was a noted big-game hunter around the turn of the century. He visited New Zealand in 1902 and, among others, was introduced to Donne, then acting in his capacity as general manager of the Department of Tourist and Health Resorts. Littledale and Donne both spoke the same language inasmuch as they considered New Zealand's wonderful high country an ideal place to liberate many types of game animals, including thar.

With great generosity the Duke of Bedford presented the New Zealand Government with a further gift of thar, six males and two females, which arrived safely in this country in 1909. Following the normal period of confinement on Somes Island (three months), they were also released in the Mount Cook area.

All 13 thar liberated at Mount Cook were bred at Woburn, the descendants of animals imported from India in 1894. Instinctively these park-bred thar would have soon familiarised themselves with their new mountain habitat. Here they could traverse dizzy heights comparable with terrain found in their native range; they could inhabit sun-filled basins and meadows, alive with tasty grasses and herbs, where no hunter had yet set foot.

In 1909 the Government also obtained three thar, one male and two females, and liberated them in what was then called the Hot Lakes District (near Lake Rotorua). Again in 1911 or 1913 (reports vary) a further release of three thar was made at Franz Josef Glacier in Westland. Evidence is curiously lacking as to where any of these animals were obtained from, and why they failed to establish themselves.

In the meantime the thar at Mount Cook, untroubled by man and only rarely seen from the Hermitage, continued to increase in numbers. In 1916 Donne, curious to know how they were faring, contacted the chief alpine guide at Mount Cook, Peter Graham. He replied that a herd of 18 or 20 animals had been seen the previous year. Donne was greatly encouraged: obviously there would be other animals in the area. Two years later a herd of at least 50 thar was spotted from the Hermitage. The last liberation of thar at Mount Cook, four animals from the Wellington zoo, took place in 1919 and by 1920 a herd of around 100 animals was observed.

Under legal protection thar not only increased greatly in numbers but they also ranged further afield. This was into country that already carried a high population of chamois and that in the past had been frequently burnt off and stocked with sheep. All these factors combined to have a devastating effect on the alpine vegetation.

In May 1929 the Waimate Acclimatisation Society held an open season for both thar and chamois. The licence cost £10. The holder could shoot two thar or two chamois but not, in the words of the society, 'exceeding two heads in all'. Three licences were offered and three were sold. In the following year, when the licence was reduced to £5, not a single application was received. The society was very doubtful that the sport would ever really take on. It was of course in that same year that matters finally came to a head for most game animals. All protection was removed. Thar were there for the taking.

In the early-to-middle 1930s photographs of successful thar hunters were not uncommon in the *Auckland Weekly News* and, although government hunters waged an unrelenting war on red deer, there was no official government action to cut back the ever-growing numbers of thar and chamois. However, Captain G. F. Yerex, who was spear-heading the Deer Control Section of the Department of Internal Affairs, knew only too well the serious threat that both thar and chamois were posing in the Mount Cook area. In a field survey in 1934 he found that there were 'well-worn tracks everywhere and erosion resulting therefrom and from the killing of protective vegetation appears imminent'.

In their Annual Report for 1936 the Department of Internal Affairs stated that hunting parties would operate in the Mount Cook locality during the forthcoming winter. In that campaign a total of 2765 thar were killed. The department reported, 'a termination of the menace these animals constitute is, it is thought, already in sight'. Surprisingly there was no follow-up operation carried out on thar by the government hunters in the following year, but in 1939 a total of 906 were eliminated.

Throughout the war years thar were largely left alone by both government and private hunters who, at that time, pursued red deer for the value of their skins (thar skins had a very low commercial value). In this period it is worth noting that thar were not looked upon with much favour by the average New Zealand hunter. They ranked far below any type of deer as either a sporting or a trophy animal.

In their Annual Report for the year ending 31 March 1948 the Department of Internal Affairs looked back on a most successful thar season: 'Operations were conducted in the Mount Cook region and excellent results were achieved

(2032 kills). It is evident that these animals are spreading and that, owing to the difficult nature of the country in which they are located, the problem of control will be a difficult one.'

But difficult country or not they could report in 1956, at which time they transferred the problem of noxious-animal control to the Forest Service, that 'the thar problem is not now considered serious and only in isolated instances does this animal cause any concern.'

In a 20-year period government shooters accounted for approximately 14,096 thar, a reasonable number considering the limited amount of time the Deer Control Section could devote to thar control. The fact that the majority of government hunters were not equipped, either mentally or physically, for hunting in such dangerous terrain also played a telling role. In effect the overall figure of recorded kills helped to keep thar numbers down, but by no stretch of the imagination did it keep up with the annual birth rate. In 1956, for instance, quite contrary to what the Department of Internal Affairs implied for that year, herds of thar, not infrequently 100-strong, could be seen quite often from the rough road leading to the Hermitage at Mount Cook. They were abundant in the heads of the big, virtually untouched river valleys on the western side of the Main Divide.

Today on the eastern side of the Main Divide the breeding range of thar extends from the Appleyard Stream at the head of the North Mathias River in the Rakaia River catchment, south to the Hunter Valley and the Dingle Burn which flows into Lake Hawea. On the western side of the Main Divide the thar breeding range extends from the Wilkinson River at the head of the Whitcombe River to the area of the Karangarua/Copland/Landsborough rivers. All

told their breeding range extends over some 1400 square miles of the most formidable terrain in the country.

Of a wandering inclination, lone bulls have been sighted and shot in many areas well beyond the previously mentioned breeding range: to the north they have been observed in the Wilberforce and Waimakariri river catchments; to the south-west in the Matukituki River; and possibly the southernmost sighting recorded was near the confluence of the Dunstan Creek and the Manuherikia River on the eastern side of the Dunstan Mountains.

Physical Description
Differing in certain characteristics from true goats, thar are beardless animals with short, evenly curved horns. In New Zealand an adult, well-conditioned bull thar resembles a North American buffalo in his general body shape. From powerfully developed shoulders, he tapers to comparatively small hindquarters. He will stand 36–42 inches high at the shoulder and his body weight will range from 250 to 300 pounds. (Anderson and Henderson, 1961, recorded bulls weighing up to 350 pounds.) A mature female, even in very good health, is dwarfed by a master bull. She may attain a shoulder height of 32–35 inches, but lacking the immensely solid shoulder construction of the male she will rarely exceed 80 pounds.

During autumn and winter the pelage of the adult male varies from dark brown to jet black, with the belly hair being much lighter (almost cream in some cases). His body hair, underlined with a super-fine, crimped wool, which provides excellent insulation, may vary in length from four to six inches. The thick hide of a freshly killed bull has been known to weigh more than 60 pounds, but as a rule weighs 40–50 pounds — a formidable load, either way. A dark dorsal stripe extends along the backbone. In summer, when the pelage fades to varying shades of grey, the bull's dorsal stripe is much more apparent. The male has a short tail.

The bull's most arresting feature is his spectacular mane or ruff. This varies in both length, ranging from 10 to 12 inches, and in colour depending on the season. At the end of summer it runs to varying shades of grey, but in time for the rutting season, when any bull wants to look his best, it has both lengthened and changed in colour to a striking reddish brown, overlaid with a coppery flame. It is magnificent. By the end of winter and certainly by early spring, it resembles a bleached white. This contrasts strikingly with the overall pelage of a particularly dark-coated male. Following that it begins to moult, as does the entire coat, and it will not grow again until the early autumn.

The female, during the autumn and winter, tends to have a more roan-coloured pelage than the male although the belly hair is similarly light, even cream in colour. In summer the female's pelage fades, sometimes to an even lighter shade than the male's coat. The female also has horns and a short tail similar to the male but does not grow a mane and neither is her body hair as long.

At birth the young are a pale light brown, a similar shade in fact to their mothers in late spring/early summer. Yearlings are a uniform greyish-brown.

Unlike deer, which both cast and then regrow their antlers on a yearly basis, thar and chamois retain the one set of horns throughout their lives. The horns start to grow

Peter Chamberlain, master alpine hunter, looking for thar using binoculars and a 20x Nikon spotting scope. Thar hunting demands a considerable amount of time simply 'glassing' for a suitable trophy.

Perhaps the most spectacular characteristic of a mature bull is his mane or ruff.

when the animal is only a few weeks old. From a heavily constructed base, which in trophy animals may measure 8½–10 inches in circumference, the horns curve upwards and outwards before cutting back to terminate in sharp tips.

A well-developed set of bull horns measures upwards of 12 inches. According to Lydekker (1910) a set in India measured 16½ inches in length. As expected, females do not grow horns to equal those of the male, they lack the same solid construction around the bases and seldom exceed eight inches in length.

To sum up, thar are designed for the country they inhabit. Their bulky shoulders are packed with hard muscle; their hooves are built for climbing — a soft, spongy inner pad contained within a hard, horny rim; their sense of balance is extraordinary; and they possess the right mental attitude to cope with a landscape where, for the most part, only the brave or foolish would dare venture.

Habitat and Habits
Although the Southern Alps, the very backbone of the South Island, exceed 10,000 feet in altitude in many places, their average height ranges between 7000 and 9000 feet. On the steeper, western slopes where the climate is more humid and the rainfall considerably heavier, the rivers are basically mountain torrents, rampaging through narrow, tortuously formed gorges towards the Tasman Sea. During this frantic journey of a mere 15 miles these West Coast rivers fall a staggering 7000 feet in altitude. East of the Main Divide the land falls away more gradually and the valleys are significantly broader. The rivers that flow through them are less boisterous, winding out to the distant coastline over wide shingle beds.

This formidable alpine heartland constitutes thar habitat. Unquestionably it represents the harshest of all New Zealand environments. Perhaps the most striking feature of thar in this country is their remarkable ability to survive such a hazardous landscape and an equally daunting climate all year round. Normal thar range in summer is from 2500 to 7000 feet and during winter below 5000 feet, but either way they are usually located on steep rocky bluff systems or near them.

To many, these steep-walled bluffs, extending around both sides of large valleys and frequently torn apart by deep gorges, appear both complex and dangerous, but to thar they are neither. They represent a retreat, a place offering a safe and comparatively sheltered bedding area. During particularly nasty weather, they may remain in such inhospitable-looking places until the weather breaks. They can find more than adequate shelter in caves and by squirming under outcrops and shelf-like ledges. When the weather improves, they move off the bluffs, following well-used routes such as extremely narrow ledges or linking terraces to well-established feeding grounds. They usually set out to feed in the late afternoon, returning to cover the following morning. The degree of hunting pressure determines with what urgency, and how soon after daybreak, this is carried out.

Unless disturbed by too much hunting pressure (and evidence suggests that thar can withstand a great deal) or by a food supply becoming exhausted, thar will remain in the same general area for a considerable length of time — several years possibly. They are, moreover, not continuous feeders, which indicates they use well whatever they partake of. Having said that, it must be stressed that they are selective feeders. Depending on the season and what altitude they are found at, their choice of food will include the various tussock grasses, mountain daisies, lilies, buttercups, snowberries, several types of hebes and sub-alpine shrubbery (which rarely grow above 3500 feet).

When the mid-summer sun is scorching the landscape, bull thar feed heavily on the high-altitude varieties of tussock grasses. The findings of Ken Tustin (1977) indicate that thar feed for around 60 per cent of the daylight hours in January. The gregarious bulls range much higher than the nannies and kids; such nursery groups appear to have an upper limit of around 5000 feet. Although we can safely say that bulls inhabit country up to 7000 feet, it is by no means unusual to see them ranging even higher than this, in particular when they are following the retreating snowline.

By and large the bulls remain together in their bachelor groups until early April when, driven by the same primeval urges that beset the male of all species, they head to lower ground, seeking out the females. The mating season extends from late April until early July. To the best of the author's knowledge the bulls do not battle amongst themselves for a female's favours, as does every other species of game animal in the country.

According to Ken Tustin, 'competition for females is decided among bulls by an intricate ritualistic repertoire of intimidation and threat displays … The displays, during which the bulls erect the mane around their head and shoulders and orientate themselves side-on to their opponents, sometimes last for an hour or more and usually result in the smaller of the contestants making a hasty retreat. Courtship involves further displays, the bull erecting his mane but remaining face-on to the female. The bull will follow the nanny for several days and stand by her in this way, often for hours on end, head and neck raised in nearly motionless poses.' Such doting attention to one female encourages the commonly held belief in this country that thar are of a monogamous nature. In areas where more than one adult female has been observed with a bull it is thought that an acute shortage of suitable bulls is the reason for it.

At any rate, the bull and nanny will spend the duration of the mating season apart from other adults. Unless she has never given birth before, the short-term family group will also include the nanny's other offspring. This might consist of a kid (now about 5–6 months old) and the issue born a year before that. Should this older animal be a male, then there is no reason for the master bull to be perturbed about it. The youngster will have no interest in mating until he is three years old (Anderson and Henderson, 1961).

The actual rutting of the thar is a decidedly low-key affair. On the bull's part there is no frantic vocalising, no tearing up the ground with slashing, sharp-edged forefeet. Rather the calmly natured bull is most content to rest; to let the others, if so inclined, feed nearby. It is all very ordered. And even if another similar-sized family group should turn up and the animals mingle together for a time, there is no friction whatsoever between the bulls. But isn't such behaviour only to be expected of a male animal that is perfectly happy to settle for one mate?

Following the rut, the bulls merge together again and quickly start for higher ground. Heavy snows will later drive them back down again and in the depths of mid-winter, after a particularly heavy snowfall, they may be observed low in creeks, either lurking about the extensive scrub cover or on the edges of extensive rockslips and rockslides. When the snowline starts to retreat, they waste little time in beginning to range higher.

Normally the females give birth to a single kid in

December (twins are not unknown in this country). Naturally cautious, the mothers do so under the cover of scrub. Surprisingly, it is not impossible for a female to conceive at about 18 months of age and give birth in her second year.

Suitable Rifles and Hunting Methods

Today's thar hunter is primarily concerned with securing a trophy bull. His requirements, insofar as a suitable calibre for this rugged customer are concerned, are entirely different from those of a Forest Service marksman on helicopter search-and-destroy missions in the mid-1980s. They shot mostly females and young animals at extremely close range. Such riflemen prefer light, highly accurate calibres with very little recoil; a particular favourite was the .22/250 Remington — a 55-grain bullet with an mv of 3730 fps.

The genuine trophy hunter, however, operates on foot, stalking his bull amidst some of the most magnificent country on earth. By any reckoning it is big country where, as likely as not, one's target is a considerable distance away. What is required is a flat-shooting calibre that retains sufficient striking energy out to at least 300 yards.

In the chapter on red deer, I mentioned that professional hunting guides Peter Chamberlain and Phil Wilson were, in the right circumstances, all in favour of magnum rifles. So too is Gary Joll, another professional hunting guide, who has probably seen more bull thar shot on the ground than anyone apart from government shooters of the Department of Internal Affairs in the 1930s–50s. His comments on suitable cartridges for bull thar are included here: 'Most of those who hunt with us are excellent shots and very familiar with their rifles. The most popular rifles are the magnums in 7 mm, and .300 Weatherby being about 30 per cent of

Philip Holden with his bull thar, which gained a Douglas Score of 40²/₈ points.

those rifles we see. The .270 we have found to be a real problem on big bull thar, particularly with the 130-grain projectile. This is simply not enough for large trophy bulls.'

Being 'very familiar' with one's rifle, as Gary put it, is possibly the most important factor determining hunting success, especially when shooting at long range. The wise thar hunter will have spent a considerable amount of time familiarising himself with the rifle that will be used. At the local rifle range, the hunter will sight it in carefully and, using the same ammunition as will be used on the hill, will know precisely where the point of impact is at 300–350 yards. In other words, the thar hunter should be prepared for a long shot should it eventuate. Although I have emphasised that a thar hunter today is often faced with downing a big-horned bull away over yonder, most bulls are shot at reasonable shooting distances, that is, under 200 yards.

In most cases the thar hunter will be using a rifle in the .270 (150-grain bullets are recommended), .308, 7x57 or .30-06 class. Fitted with a scope — a 4x–6x is a sound bet — and sighted in for the normal 200 yards, there is no reason why the marksman cannot make a clean, one-shot kill. Naturally equipment includes binoculars. A pair of 7x35s, 7x50s or 8x30s is an excellent choice. Philip Wilson slings a big, bulky pair of Russian-made 12x40s around his neck and gets by very well with them. A 20x spotting scope is another must for the serious trophy hunter, allowing an accurate assessment of a bull's horns from a considerable distance. (With binoculars, one cannot be quite sure if it is a bull with 12-inch horns or a beast not quite good enough in the horn department.)

A thar hunter must also be something of a mountaineer. After all he is in pursuit of an animal possessing legendary climbing ability. One has to witness at first hand the climbing expertise of thar to appreciate it fully. Either climbing or descending they can surmount near vertical rock faces with uncanny dexterity. Even that trimly built, sure-footed, Austrian high-country dweller — the chamois — rates a distant second. In times of peril thar will simply, as it were, step off the edge of the world. They will descend from one tiny ledge to another, each leap or jump perfectly timed. In mid-air their legs are often outstretched, braced, their hair drifting back. Seen from below they do in fact appear to float — a parachutist in free fall. In this manner, with each leap covering as much as 30 feet, they can descend 1000 feet or more in a very short time. It is breathtaking and certainly contributes to their standing as one of the world's great game animals. The sensible thar hunter will of course not try to emulate it!

The very nature of thar country demands that one does not hunt alone. I couldn't think of a worse place to fall and break a leg on your own more than 6000 feet up on ice-blocked bluffs in the middle of winter. Also, a high degree of physical fitness is required. The intelligent thar hunter, in preparing for his trip, will have included plenty of hill-work in his solid training programme, and the steeper it is the better. Boots must be strongly constructed, offer ample support to the ankles, and be fitted with tricounis — five or six to each boot, depending on individual choice. In winter crampons and ice axe are a must, as is a length of nylon rope. Gary Joll considers it should be approximately 100 feet in length and have a breaking strain greater than 1000 pounds. As he says, 'Such a rope is invaluable in river crossing, or in negotiating very difficult rock faces or ice slopes and has saved many a life in alpine accidents.'

No matter what the season, one must expect nasty weather. At all times woollen and windproof clothing suitable for high altitudes are essential. A change of socks makes sense. So too does a pair of sunglasses, especially in snowy conditions. Since many trophy thar hunts turn into lengthy affairs — daylight to dusk is not unusual — some high-energy food and something to drink must be taken. A torch should not be overlooked either. And all of this goes into a stout day-pack. In short, then, today's bull thar hunter is very much a specialist and the more attention paid to details, the greater the chance of success.

Unless a trophy bull is located in a creek bottom or within easy shooting range of it — not at all unusual when winter snows drive them to low levels — the usual pattern of a thar hunt is as follows: from a good vantage point, such as a rocky outcrop 500–800 feet above the main creek, you start glassing all the likely spots. It is a slow, methodical, systematic process of elimination until a trophy is found. If it isn't found then another similar position, offering an entirely different view, of a side creek perhaps, is chosen. Then the same routine starts all over again. It is tiring on one's eyes, so it is essential that field glasses be perfectly aligned otherwise severe eyestrain will result. In other words, serious thar hunting isn't about climbing to high ground in the hope of blundering upon a bull with trophy-length horns. No, you first find your bull before climbing in earnest. That's the way the professional guides do it, and in the 1980s they've produced the big heads to prove that it pays off.

Let's say that we've at least spotted a good bull. Up on those craggy bluffs, 2500 feet higher, he won't be easy to take. Again it might be too late in the day to attempt it. Not to worry: he'll be in the same general vicinity tomorrow. The only problem with having to delay a hunt until the next day is the weather. The following morning might bring a snowstorm or driving rain. No one in their right mind will try to find a thar in such conditions. Apart from its being too

dangerous, that bull will have gone to ground, snug in his long-haired coat under a concealing rocky ledge.

The usual method of stalking a bull thar is to climb to the same level or, better still, a little above, and then with the utmost care to sidle towards him. Every bit of natural cover must be used. Thar have keen eyesight, particularly when it comes to movement. Other animals must always be taken into consideration, too; spook them and that might be your lot. The wind can also be tricky, but once above an animal its general flow is normally advantageous. Thar and other game animals are seldom concerned with what's above them; animals on the alert in high country invariably face downhill, into the wind. Finally, great care must be taken, when closing in for the kill, not to dislodge any small stones or, worse, large rocks. A minor avalanche is the very last thing any thar hunter needs after making a long and arduous stalk.

All things being equal, a bull thar is not a particularly difficult animal to kill. Thousands have been shot with .303s and many with .243s and the like. But tally-hunting for the government is not trophy hunting. The difference is as great as that between a mature bull thar and an adult female thar. Trophy hunting necessitates putting down the animal where it is standing. No government culler I've heard of ever lost sleep because a trophy bull pitched over a bluff and broke a 13-inch horn in half. He was after tails, not heads. But to an Australian or North American client of a professional hunting guide, it is a mind-shattering experience after several days of arduous hunting to watch a hard-hit trophy bull lurch about and then stagger a few fatal yards before pitching headlong into space, to fall perhaps 500 feet. Quite often such bulls are impossible to retrieve. This is particularly so in mid-winter when snow and, in particular, ice make conditions extremely dangerous.

The Perilous Situation

Bull thar, monarch of all he surveys

Peter Chamberlain confidently climbs up the formidable terrain of Waterfall Gorge.

With amazing agility the thar, a big female with a long, shaggy coat, bolted straight up what appeared to be a perpendicular rockface. It was just one of a series of near vertical bluffs practically overhanging the Macauley River in Canterbury. With her spring-loaded hoofs as effective as a climber's crampons, and infinitely more versatile, she reached a patch of sun-warmed shingle. She sped across it, dislodging a number of rocks. They hurtled out into space, speeding like missiles towards the man directly below.

Scrambling around a narrow ledge, Lance Barnard, on a thar photographic assignment for the Forest Service, was aware now that he had badly underestimated the nature of the terrain. The ground under his feet resembled an ice rink, the bluffs were much steeper than he'd anticipated from the river bottom: leaving his crampons with his pack had been a terrible mistake. Another rock flashed past Lance's tense face; it might have been hurled in anger. He saw with a tight smile that the thar had stopped on the skyline. She was well within range of his 300 mm Zuiko telephoto lens. With the sun falling on her, she would, Lance knew, make a wonderful subject. Quickly he raised his camera.

Suddenly he lost his balance on the slippery ground. In an attempt to regain it, he whipped back his right arm and with brute force struck out above his head with a short-handled ice-axe. No use. The sharp point of the tool merely bounced off the flint-like rockface; the jarring impact sent shock waves racing from his wrist to his elbow. He cursed furiously as he started to slip backwards. The realisation that he was about to fall exploded like a shellburst in his panic-stricken mind.

Both below and above him was a narrow chute. On either side of it were bluffs remarkably similar to those the thar had just traversed. Within the chute was a frozen waterfall — a sheet of ice glittering in the sun. It started about 60 metres above him and ended about half that distance below. Mostly it fell in a series of short drops, with each one separated by a narrow ledge. In effect, and particularly from afar, it might easily have resembled a giant, watery staircase.

By the time Lance struck the first ledge he was already falling at an alarming rate. He heard himself cry out. Desperately he tried with a slashing, sideways blow to check himself with his ice-axe, but the lightweight tool, attached to his right wrist by a nylon strap, made no impression on the frozen rockface.

Like a falling stone he plummeted down the next straight drop, a distance of about three metres. Then, lurching like a drunken man on the next ledge, he thought for one deceiving instant that he had successfully lodged the tip of his ice-axe in a tiny crevice. Then he was falling once more, threatening to topple over backwards, to spill out into space, arms akimbo, in spectacular freefall. But somehow he remained upright in his terrifying descent. His telephoto lens, swinging back and forth crazily on his strap round his neck, thudded against his chest like blows from a fist. He felt his feet shoot out from beneath him. His gloveless hands, already bleeding profusely, clawed ineffectually for a firm grip on the glassy surface of the ice.

Below the falling man was just one more ledge; beyond that a 500-metre drop to the river bottom. This ledge was wider than those above it, flatter too. Also it was well studded with rocks of various sizes — gleaming lumps locked to the ground by ice. Lance struck this last ledge hard. His knees buckled; he fell to the ground. Immediately he started to slide towards the edge. Frantically he grabbed at an ice-crusted lump. His hands formed a death-like grip about it. Despite its small size, the rock held firm. With a choked sob he realised that he was less than two metres from the edge. He half turned so that he was able to look over his shoulder. Trembling he saw the river: it looked far away. He also saw a green speck near the water's edge, his mountain mule pack. He shuddered.

Lance didn't know how long he lay there hugging the ground or, for that matter, what time it had been when he had fallen. What he did know was that the sun had vanished and that he was numb with cold. Also the thumb of his bruised right hand was throbbing so badly he wondered if he had broken it. Shakily he climbed to his feet. He felt groggy, light-headed. Everything seemed a little unreal, a little out of focus. He forced himself with enormous difficulty not to look down. He raised his eyes and looked to where he had fallen from; a distance, he judged, of around 30 to 40 metres. His mind flooded with despair: without crampons there was absolutely no way he could climb out of here. The bluffs on either side of the chute formed an awesome overhang. In the late afternoon there was a strange bluish tinge over the entire rockface. He shivered. In an oddly detached manner he realised that he had just uttered a child-like whimper of fear.

On that same August day in 1982 Lance had arrived at Lilybank station, near Lake Tekapo. There he'd sought out Gary Joll and Ron Spanton. Gary looked after the world-famous hunting reserve on the property; Ron was in charge of stock operations. Twice before they had given him permission to cross station land and make his way up the nearby Macauley River to Waterfall hut; the station men camped there when they were mustering.

Before he had left, Gary had kidded Lance that if he wasn't out in three weeks — the length of time Lance had given himself for this trip — they'd come looking for his frozen body. Now, in a seemingly hopeless situation, Lance reflected grimly on those lightly spoken words of Gary's. His mind turned to his wife and their two young children in Wellington. A mistake. He started to sob.

By now Lance's corduroy jeans were frozen solid from the knee down. He longed for the warmth of his bulky, down-filled jacket. But that was a long way below him. He knew that in less than 90 minutes it would be fully dark. If he wasn't off these bluffs by then it would be all over. A search party would indeed be searching for his body. The impact of that was too enormous for him to fully comprehend.

In recalling this incident, Lance remembered that an inner voice started to scream at him then: that he had to make a move; that it would be best for him to attempt the bluff to his right rather than trying to climb where he had fallen. And that, above all else, he had to believe that the sickening drop below him was more like five or six metres than the distance it really was. Suddenly he felt much calmer, rational. He gulped air into his lungs and with care lodged the toe of his boot in a minute cranny. He found a grip for the unfeeling tips of his fingers. He started to climb.

Sobbing with relief, he eventually found himself back on the narrow ledge from where he had fallen. Following that, he soon reached safe ground and in the dusk, the river bottom.

On further trips into the same area, Lance would pause below where all this had happened. He would look up at the waterfalls and the bluffs hemming it in and every time he would experience a sick feeling in the pit of his stomach. How on earth, he would wonder, had he managed to find it in himself to surmount such a formidable obstacle?

'It was the first time I
had seen thar in a
perfectly natural
setting; the reality was
infinitely better than
I could have possibly
imagined.'
— *Philip Holden.*

Hunt South — 1989

Preface

It was a magnificent mid-August evening as I drove through the Lindis Valley in Otago after what had been a wonderful day. Starting at Te Anau, I had driven through Queenstown, Cromwell, and Tarras, enchanted by a constant visual delight.

A signpost flashed by — Morven Hills Station. Although I had never visited this famous old property, the name was as familiar to me as it is to anyone deeply interested in the story of how red deer were introduced into New Zealand.

Presently I reached Lindis Pass (1006 metres) and pulled over to a layby where a simple stone cairn stood. Suitably inscribed, it had been erected 17 years ago by the Otago branch of the NZDA to commemorate a significant event that had taken place a century earlier.

Turning away from the cairn, I crossed the road and looked back the way I had just come. Patches of snow lay in low, sheltered gullies and introduced sweet briar flanked much of the slopes. There wasn't a single tree in sight. The tussocky tops were now a deep tawny gold — an almost unreal colour — and I doubted if they could ever appear more stunning. Reluctant to leave, I wondered what impact such a view would have had on the young Scotsman, John MacLean. In the winter of 1858, he had dismounted from his horse in this pass and looked westwards, down into what we call the valley of the Lindis River.

John MacLean hailed from the Isle of Coll, off the west coast of Scotland. Forced to leave because of famine, 22-year-old John, his mother and two brothers set sail for Lyttelton. At first, the MacLeans took up land at what today is known as MacLeans' Island on the south bank of the Waimakariri River in Canterbury. In 1855, they acquired an 18,600-hectare property inland from Ashburton, but not even this was big enough for the wildly ambitious Scotsman.

By all accounts it was a wandering Maori chief named Huruhuru who first told John MacLean of the vast grasslands of the Otago hinterland. No white man, with the possible exception of James McKenzie (of sheep-stealing notoriety), had ever gazed upon this land. To MacLean it sounded ideal sheep country, the opportunity he had been waiting for.

With Huruhuru as guide, MacLean crossed the Lindis Pass and pressed on towards the west. From a high point, later named Mount Grandview, MacLean was able to look over a stupendous tract of mostly open land. Here was a kingdom of grass — his for the taking! In high excitement, MacLean returned home. On 5 September 1858, he and the other three members of his family were granted a licence to lease over 200,000 hectares for 14 years. John called what is thought to be the largest single holding ever known in this country 'Morven Hills'.

By the mid-1860s there were around 20,000 sheep on the property, and by 1871 this figure had increased dramatically to 110,000. Convoys of up to five wagons, each pulled by teams of 12 or 14 bullocks, were used to transport the mighty wool clip through the Lindis Pass to the port of Oamaru. The return trip, in excess of 320 kilometres, could take as long as three weeks.

On 20 October 1870, the *City of Dunedin* set sail from London. On board were eight five-month-old red deer calves — two males and six females. They, and nine other calves of similar age which were shipped on the *Warrior Queen* on 29 November, came from the famed deer forest of Invermark, Forfarshire. The Otago Acclimatisation Society was to be the fortunate recipient of such fine stock.

The *Otago Daily Times* of 27 February 1871 reported how

the calves shipped on the *Warrior Queen* had fared on the trip to Port Chalmers:

> *... of the nine red deer shipped, which*
> *constituted the remainder of the lot presented*
> *to the Society by Lord Dalhousie, none had been*
> *lost. They have arrived in splendid condition, and*
> *those in charge state that they are growing so*
> *fast, that had the voyage lasted a month longer,*
> *larger boxes would have had to be constructed*
> *for them ...*

These nine red deer calves were taken to Bushey Park, near Palmerston.

Of the eight on the *City of Dunedin*, only six survived the journey. They were initially taken to Oamaru by paddle-steamer, and from there transported up the Waitaki Valley by bullock wagons belonging to Morven Hills station.

I tried to imagine them now — 117 years later — eventually reaching the Lindis Pass. The well-used route would have been deeply rutted, but most likely dry as it was early autumn. Certainly after the long haul up to the actual pass they must have rested the teams of bullocks. Perhaps even Big Jock, as John MacLean was known by then, was there to supervise everything.

Once in the Lindis Pass, the yearlings would have seen a landscape remarkably like the high, wild place where they had been born. A fitting place, indeed, to liberate Scotland's grandest game animal in March 1871. The inscription on the NZDA cairn states that these deer 'formed the basis of the world renowned Otago-South Westland red deer herd'.

It was, I noticed, becoming colder in the Lindis Pass.

Red deer spiker.

Time to move on, yet I was oddly reluctant to leave this awesomely beautiful spot. Heavy dark shadows were creeping insidiously up the mountain flanks and the sun, almost below the horizon, was still catching the clear-cut peaks.

Yes, I thought, the story of red deer in this part of the country had really started here. I shook my head, thinking back to 1961 when I had first arrived in New Zealand. Who would have thought back then that deer farming would be a reality before the sixties were out? Or that a million deer could be behind high wire by 1990?

The Australian Story: Crocodile — 1993

To Die Like a Warrior

The adult saltwater crocodile is easy to recognise because of its broad snout.

A white-chested sea eagle and its kill.

*T*hat big crocodile, he has just been waiting for someone to swim across. He has been hanging around, taking dogs and watching people for some months now. We are pretty shocked, but not really surprised. Borroloola Aboriginal woman, Linda Mowson, in the aftermath of a fatal crocodile attack in the McArthur River, September 1986.

While Raymond John had survived a crocodile attack in the McArthur River at Borroloola in the May of 1985, it wasn't until 16 months later that crocodile warning signs were erected on the banks of the river.

Compared with other major rivers in the Top End, the McArthur, while still offering the species excellent habitat, was considered by the Conservation Commission rangers to support smaller numbers of saltwater crocodiles. Smaller, but no less lethal.

Even before Raymond John was mauled, locals had known, for quite some time, that a particularly large crocodile was inhabiting the river close to town. It was often seen near the boat ramp at Rocky Point Landing, a popular fishing location. At this point the river was about 40 metres (130 feet) wide by 8 metres (26 feet) deep.

Some of the older Aborigines in the district believed that the crocodile had lived in the waterways of the river for over fifty years; that he might have been sixty years old.

In any event, the crocodile was so well known by locals that they had even given him a name: Gus. It is of course debatable whether Gus would have chosen such a name for himself.

In returning to the Raymond John incident, it is thought that the crocodile which attacked him was of medium size, that is, about 3.5 metres (11 feet 5 inches). While no one had ever measured Gus, he was certainly much bigger than that. Given that Gus resided in the area where John was attacked, we cannot rule out the distinct possibility that he was the villain after all. The thing is, anyone who was drunk enough to swim in the McArthur River after dark wouldn't have known whether they were attacked by a 3.5-metre crocodile or a 4-metre grey nurse shark.

Following the initial newspaper reports about the Raymond John incident, word spread around town that not only had he attempted to swim the river after dark, but he'd actually taken a crate of beer with him. Presumably, John did not intend to use that as a life raft in case he got into difficulties.

This incredible revelation, however, explains precisely why the crocodile, after taking John with a firm grip about the chest and upper shoulder, decided to let him go. It fancied a beer instead! Who knows, old Gus or some young, unnamed crocodile might have taken off in glee with that crate of beer, just like Baru on the Cato River had done with a flour bin, and taken it to a hidey-hole. Not that your run-of-the-mill McArthur River crocodile would have invited its scaly-backed mates around for a booze up, you understand. Crocs aren't into mateship!

Anyway, in direct line with their policy of removing large and therefore potentially dangerous crocodiles from well-frequented areas, Conservation Commission rangers, only too aware of Gus's presence at Borroloola, had decided he was a prime target for relocation. Again Gus did not have any say in the matter, but we may assume that somewhere else to live at his age would not have been of his choosing. The stress factor alone would quite easily have killed him.

Accordingly, then, a steel-mesh trap was set for our boy. But traps come in all sizes. The one the rangers placed in

While it may appear to be serene, this lovely billabong is likely to be the habitat of a large crocodile.

the McArthur River proved much too small for him from the evidence they found of where he had tried to enter it. How big was Gus? Certainly over 4 metres (13 feet)!

By the time the crocodile warning signs had gone up on 9 September, the rangers had yet to replace the trap with a larger one. On Tuesday, 9 September, readers of the *Northern Territory News* were faced with this sobering headline:

Big Gulf Hunt for Killer Croc

And below those chilling words 'Killer Croc' they read:

> *A crack Conservation Commission wildlife team will start searching the McArthur River at Borroloola tonight for a crocodile that savaged a Queensland man.*

Since the *Northern Territory News* comes out in the

Feral pigs roam in large numbers across most of Australia and make a welcome feed for a crocodile.

afternoon, no one was put off their breakfast.

The 'Queensland man' in the above paragraph was Rusty Wherret, 39, of Mareeba. A somewhat itinerant type, Wherret was a fencing contractor who had been working in the district prior to the attack. On the previous Saturday night, he and his mate, Dennis Vowken, had put in plenty of elbow bending in one of the town's pubs. They stayed there by all accounts until closing. Used to roughing it, they decided to camp in the open rather than stay in a hotel.

So they drove on down to the river at Rocky Point Landing. Maybe the lights of their vehicle momentarily illuminated the crocodile warning signs; maybe not.

Around daybreak, Dennis Vowken awoke in his swag. His mate wasn't in his bedroll — what the hell? Vowken staggered unsteadily to his feet, his head pounding. Hey, what was this? Rusty's shirt, which he had been wearing last night, was lying as though cast away at the water's edge.

According to the newspaper reports, Dennis Vowken '... did not alert the police until several hours later because he believed his friend had gone for a walk'.

A walk seems a highly unlikely deduction. A swim was more likely. Still, both men had had a great deal to drink, and that does not make for clear and logical thinking around first light the following day.

Once the police were notified of Wherret's disappearance, Constables Mal Jensen and Rex Grass went for a stroll upstream of Rocky Point Landing. They were both of the opinion that sometime during the night Wherret had gone for a swim and, being under the effects of too much alcoholic beverage, had drowned. If they did not locate the missing man's body today, then it would undoubtedly turn up later.

Barramundi form a large part of a crocodile's diet in some billabongs.

'Everyone in town knew you must never swim in the river.'

They were about 100 metres from the boat ramp when they realised the horrible truth.

The news that the police had found two severed legs on the river bank near Rocky Point Landing rocked sleepy little Borroloola. Some locals, perhaps without giving it real thought, reckoned 'the man had asked for it'. Linda Mowson, among other succinct comments, said, 'Everyone in town knew you must never swim in the river.'

Well, we can think of a couple of examples of folks who didn't know that.

On the night of 9 September, having arrived earlier that day from Darwin, the Conservation Commission's crack crocodile-hunting team were going through their well-practised paces on the McArthur River. They were Bryan Walsh, Bill Binns, Phil Hauser and Ross Bryan. They concentrated their efforts that first night in and around the area of Rocky Point Landing.

Next day, the *Northern Territory News* reported:

> **Suspect Crocodile Spotted**
> *Conservation Commission searchers believe they may have found the crocodile which ate a man in the McArthur River at Borroloola on Sunday.*
> *The rangers got within about 8 metres of the crocodile but were not in a position to trap it.*

Interesting, if somewhat gruesome, details pertaining to the rangers' search for the mankiller were written by Inspector Maurie Burke, Northern Territory Police, and published in an edition of the *Australian Police Journal*. Particularly relevant is the section relating to how the rangers actually located Gus.

'It was highly likely he was the culprit. This was partially confirmed by the particularly putrid stench of his breath. Whilst patrolling for him the officers, whether they could see him or not, were aware of his presence by the stench of his breath.

'Even submerged the bubbles expelled were putrid enough to cause near-vomiting by officers if they were caught unaware leaning from the boat and having the bubbles burst in their faces.'

Well, no one ever said that a wildlife officer's lot was perfect.

On the second night of the hunt for Gus, the rangers, because of the noise factor, decided to use a silent-running electric motor powered by a battery, rather than the comparatively noisy outboard motor normally in use.

They were close to the boat ramp when, in the words of Bryan Walsh, 'Suddenly we picked up a set of red eyes in the spotlight, right where the remains were found. It was then we knew we were onto the right croc.'

They moved closer to the crocodile. In went the harpoon, just above the back leg.

Bryan Walsh: 'We had to stay with the croc. It was smart enough to swim through every bit of snag and tree it could find. After two hours of following it, we got really close. We shot it in the head and brought it in for autopsy.'

The remains of Rusty Wherret were found inside Gus. According to Inspector Burke, 'The digestive juices had already reduced bone matter to the consistency of rubbery gristle, flesh to a jelly-like substance and skin bleached and rubbery in texture. From the bruising sustained to the hands and arms it was evident that Wherret was alive when it happened. It would appear that he was taken from behind, crushed through the middle by the immense power of the jaws. Whilst struggling to escape, his arms and hands were lacerated and punctured by the crocodile's teeth.

'He was carried upstream for 100 metres before the final "death-roll" and flailing of the now-lifeless body severed the arms and legs.'

Which naturally explains how Wherret's legs ended up high and dry on the bank.

A few pithy comments relating to Gus were served up by Bryan Walsh: 'His age is fairly hard to estimate because crocs grow rapidly and then slow up, and a lot is dependent on the conditions and food supply. This big one was in very good condition, although it had a part of its tail missing and numerous other scars.'

Even with some of his tail missing, Gus measured 4.5 metres (14 feet 7 inches). It was estimated that with his tail intact he would have stretched out to 5.1 metres (16 feet 6 inches). He measured just over 2 metres (6 feet 6 inches) around the girth and had an 'estimated' weight of between 800 kilograms and a tonne (1760–2200 pounds).

So Gus was not destined to spend the remainder of his life on a crocodile farm. Perhaps it is just as well that that was the way of it, that it was right and proper that he should go out fighting in his own territory. Better to die like a warrior than wither like a coward.

From that moment long ago when he had emerged from an egg he had been an aggressive predator, foraging for himself, asking no favours, fighting his own battles. And somehow, because he was one of the chosen ones, he had survived to live his life along the waterways of the McArthur River.

A hundred years from now they will still talk about Gus in Borroloola, for crocodiles, just like man, can become immortal too.

The Australian Story: Crocodile — 1993

Will the Real Sweetheart Please Stand Up?

Saltwater crocodile — last of the ruling reptiles.

He was such an old croc — belted up, face mauled, no arm: I mean he was one mangled up croc. The fact this croc has got so many scars makes me think he is the real Sweetheart and even Graham Webb said it was quite likely. George Craig, Green Island, talking about a captive crocodile, Cassius, trapped in the same general region where the legendary Sweetheart made his name.

'And this is Cassius,' said George Craig with obvious pride.

We were standing in the noon sun at Marineland Melanesia on Green Island, which is off the coast of Cairns.

'He doesn't come out of the water much,' George added.

'Not today, anyway,' I said drily.

George smiled. 'Right.'

In fact, all that could be seen of Cassius was a bit of his snout and one yellowish eye.

'How old is he?'

George ran splayed fingers through his greyish beard. 'Hard to say really.' He paused. 'But at a rough guess I'd say ninety.'

Ninety?

I mulled that over. Even at that great age, Cassius would still be growing. Ninety? If George was right about that, then Cassius was born in 1902. He came from the Finniss River in the Northern Territory. 1902? My word, it was truly a 'territory' then. In these days of strict gun control, it is difficult to believe how lax gun laws were then. Territorians were as well armed as their North American counterparts on their frontiers. Territorians, a hard-bitten bunch, wore holstered Colt revolvers and sheathed Bowie knives on their belts, carried Winchester rifles or carbines, mostly calibre .44/40. Some of them in the early 1890s were not above shooting at blacks for target practice. For their part the blacks, not to be outdone, retaliated by seeing just how deep one of their long-range, shovel-nosed spears could penetrate a white man. The consensus was deep enough.

As George and I stood there, soaking up the sun and talking in general about crocodiles (actually, I was doing most of the listening), several well-dressed Japanese tourists, no doubt wondering what was holding our attention, also looked into Cassius' enclosure. Typically, they appeared so cool and collected that they might just have stepped out of an ice-cold shower. Still, downtown Tokyo offered anyone intending to visit North Queensland a good training ground in high humidity.

The Japanese looked at what little could be seen of Cassius. For his part, Cassius stared back … what was he thinking? Losing interest, they moved to another pen, in which was Oscar. Unlike Cassius, he was completely out of the water, lying on the concrete surrounds of his pen like a beached whale. You get the idea: he was bigger than big.

But for now let us turn our attention away from Cassius and Oscar and, for a few moments, concentrate on George Craig. In the early 1950s he had hunted crocodiles for a living in the Top End, mostly on the Adelaide River. He was 22 years old then, fit and muscular. Later, he had carried on the same profession in New Guinea.

Today, George is considerably older, but he still looks fit and tough. Darn good in fact for a man on the far side of sixty.

George and Shirley Craig had remained on Daru Island (Papua New Guinea) until 1972. George would have been quite happy to stay there, meandering up the Fly River with his good-natured crew, shooting and trapping crocodiles. Trouble was, political unrest on a grand scale was sweeping

New Guinea then. European crocodile hunters were as welcome as a fox in a chicken coop. Even as late as the early 1970s there were still tribes in that neck of the woods who made darn sure the ancient sport of headhunting wasn't a dying art. Dying being the operative word, you understand. And while it was true most of these types were confined to the highlands, and not along the banks of the Fly, well, you never really knew, did you?

So it was time to quit New Guinea. A pity, but there it was. Back home to Australia then — not easy after 15 years away. But back to the rest of the family. What about Oscar?

To put you in the picture, he had been captured in 1967 well up the Fly, lured from a deep pool with a bait few crocs can resist: a pig's head. It was attached to the end of a length of strong rope and, rather unfairly, there was a solid hook in the tempting package too.

Oscar measured 5.48 metres (17 feet 9 inches) and weighed over a tonne (2200 pounds).

Interestingly, George and his team had captured an even bigger crocodile up the Fly — a full 5.95 metres (19 feet 4 inches) in length. It had given them a tremendous battle before they managed to subdue it and drag it from the river onto a mudbank, where it soon died. That type of thing, George recalls today, can damn near kill you too.

By the early 1990s, the Craigs had about 40 crocodiles all up, including another big bruiser called Gomik who, at 5.33 metres (17 feet 4 inches), also weighed in at over a tonne. When George was off on his regular forays up the Fly, it was his wife's responsibility to look after them all. They were kept in rather rickety pens: your typical New

A smaller Australian reptile: the 'bearded dragon'.

Feeding time for Zac at Wild World.

Guinea crocodile cage. And given time, Oscar settled down there. Which isn't the same thing, George reckons, as being tamed. You can't tame a crocodile to the point, for instance, where you can trust it: a crocodile's brain does not function that way.

In his pen, Oscar put on weight. Oscar wasn't having to forage for himself any more — meals were laid on. Consequently, he gave the impression that he had slowed up and become a fat, lazy sort of crocodile. Wrong. He was just the same crocodile that had lived for around 50 years in the Fly River, until a man had come along with a baited pig's head.

Beneath that veneer was the same old Oscar. While you can take a crocodile away from the wild, you really cannot take the wild away from a crocodile.

On occasions pigeons would alight in Oscar's pen. Foolishly, they would walk closer and still closer to the huge reptile, which seemed to all intents and purposes to be as dead as that stuffed celebrity in the Northern Territory Museum of Arts and Sciences in Darwin. But Oscar knew how to come alive in a real big hurry. Suddenly, there would be a flash of movement and a distinct chomping sound. While a few feathers may have fluttered up in the air, you could be quite certain that the pigeon wasn't around any more. Oscar became rather partial to pigeon pie during that period of his life.

The description of Oscar that George offered — that is, slow and fat and lazy — would have fitted very well perhaps a certain saltwater crocodile that was unfortunate enough to end up in a zoo in Sri Lanka. It was a big crocodile — a good 4.3 metres (13 feet 11 inches). It lived in a tiny pen, in which was a trough of water about 5 metres (16 feet) long by 2 metres (6½ feet) wide and, say, one metre (3 feet) deep. Something like you or I lying in a conventional bath — no swimming room, in other words.

Anyway, the crocodile had been there for around five years when an adult Langur monkey, a type noted for extreme agility, escaped from its cage, which happened to be close to the crocodile's pen. The monkey raced into the crocodile's pen and paused momentarily, as if to gather its bearings. Now the crocodile in all likelihood hadn't made a sudden, aggressive move in all those five years. Even so, just like Oscar, its instincts were sharply honed, as finely tuned as though it too were still existing in the wild. As the monkey hesitated, the crocodile launched itself out of the trough. Like the crocodile, the monkey also possessed hair-trigger reactions. Sensing the danger, it sprang into the air, but too late — the crocodile had it. A big gulp and a swallow and that was that. Lying in its trough that crocodile, because of its big, exposed tooth, the fourth in the lower jaw, might have appeared to be smiling. Most likely he was — after all, there had been precious little for it to grin about since it had been cooped up there five long years ago.

But back to Oscar.

Naturally, the crocodiles that the Craigs kept penned on Daru Island were a big attraction for locals and visitors alike. I mean, where else could you see in captivity a couple of crocodiles in excess of 5 metres (16 feet)?

One day a French Canadian bishop of a rather portly build arrived to see the crocodiles. George, of course, was delighted when His Eminence turned up. He took the bishop on a grand tour and presently reached Oscar's pen. Oscar, as you will have gathered, was truly George's pride and joy.

The bishop listened while George explained where Oscar had come from and how they had captured him.

'Could be the biggest croc in captivity,' George said, his manner that of a proud father watching his son excel at sport.

Nodding, the bishop listened.

Then, for a moment, George's attention was diverted and, while his back was turned, an incredible thing happened: the bishop, like a man possessed, grabbed a long bamboo pole which they used to feed the crocodiles with. He then lunged at Oscar, and with great force, for he was a heavy-set man, rammed it into the crocodile's side. Again he did so, while yelling:

'Take that!'

Crunch!

'And that! Damn you …!'

Momentarily stunned by what was happening, George then rushed to stop it: didn't the damn fool know that if he continued to do that—

Oscar had had enough. Rearing up, he hurled himself at the enraged bishop. It was just as well for the bishop's sake that a wooden partition separated them. Over a tonne of maddened crocodile hit that structure so hard it very nearly gave way. Simultaneously, the gaping jaws closed, snapping together only a matter of inches from the bishop's chest.

Two shades paler than white the bishop, crying now with fear, fell over backwards and sprawled in a most undignified manner on the dirty ground with his heavy robes cascading about him.

In recalling this most extraordinary incident, George says: 'Maybe he thought Oscar was the Devil?' If that were the case, then, had Oscar's jaws grabbed him, they would surely have been the very gates of Hell!

All this of course had taken place years ago, before they put Daru Island behind them and set up house on another lovely island, this one off the North Queensland coast. They would always remember Daru Island, though. How could they ever forget it? George, for instance, sold 29,000 crocodile skins while he was there, many of which he had bought from the locals.

On Green Island they had leased 1.35 acres, some of which had been set up as an aquarium. It was very run-down. However, there were facilities for saltwater crocodiles, and there were two very rather sad-looking crocodiles in residence. This explains why Oscar was transported to Green Island (not that he couldn't have got there under his own steam, given half the chance). Or more likely back to his own real territory: the upper Fly River, where the barramundi grew to record size and wild pigs watered incautiously.

Just two years later, Queensland at last called an end to professional crocodile hunting.

Over a cup of tea and chocolate biscuits, provided by Shirley Craig, George had been telling me all this, and the conversation had continued as we'd had a quick look at Cassius and, now, as we looked at Oscar.

As I have already said, Oscar, unlike Cassius, was right out of the water, at the very edge of his pen. All 5.48 metres (17 feet 9 inches) of him; his girth was enormous. The very idea of having a crocodile that size take to you was not a thought to linger on.

Instead, I considered Oscar's pen, a mere 15 metres (49 feet) by 5 metres (16 feet) in overall size. He had been in captivity 25 years now. I wondered what he'd give for a decent swim in the Fly River, the opportunity to submerge himself completely in deep water? I looked at George pointedly and put it to him that maybe, just maybe, Oscar's pen was on the small size. Dangerous ground?

At that, George looked a touch annoyed. He said flatly,

'You know, a lot of people ask me that. They say "Is it cruel being kept in such a relatively small area by himself?" and I say, no, it isn't. In the wild a big croc like Oscar who is getting on in years would just as likely remain in a small pool for years — that is, if he has a plentiful supply of food …' He paused. 'Not that that's always a consideration.' He left that hanging there …

'How'd you mean?'

'A croc can last nine months without food; did you know that?'

I shook my head to indicate I didn't.

'Fair enough — not many people do.' Again he paused. 'There's something else too. If I put any crocodile in there less than, say, two metres, he'd kill it.'

'And any bigger than that,' I put in, 'and they'd be battling it out because of territory.'

'Right. Don't worry about old Oscar — he's happy enough in there.'

Well, maybe Oscar was and maybe Oscar wasn't. I'd still bet that, given the choice, he'd have fancied the opportunity to propel himself with his tail through the water at a fast clip, to catch a barramundi, and dine on pork he had captured himself. Being fed a chicken every second day doesn't do a great deal for any saltwater crocodile's self-esteem.

Gesturing at Oscar, I said, 'And you say Cassius is even bigger than he is?' I was not being sceptical, merely offering a comment.

George bobbed his head. 'Uh-huh. A fair bit bigger, too.' He nodded at some passing tourists and then gave me a grin. 'Suppose you'd like to see him out of the water.'

'Had crossed my mind,' I admitted.

'Better find something for him to eat then,' George said.

While George ambled off to do just that, I moved back to

The mighty Oscar.

where Cassius was contained. His pen was shady and while his pool wasn't large — a miniature billabong — he could move around it easily.

Cassius was still in the same position — almost all his body was below the water, suspended as though in limbo.

Cassius was first brought to George Craig's attention when Hilton Graham, now crocodile farming south of Darwin, came to Green Island to look at the crocodiles — Oscar particularly — and to meet George Craig.

During the flow of their conversation, Hilton said that he'd got a really big crocodile called Cassius at his place. The word 'big' made George's ears stand up like those of a startled 'roo.

'How big?'

'Pretty big,' Hilton replied.

'Where'd he come from?'

'Finniss River.'

'Ah, Sweetheart's territory!'

'Right. In fact the Conservation Commission boys captured it pretty much where Sweetheart lived.'

George pursed his lips. 'What's your reason for selling it?'

Hilton shrugged and then explained that because of other commitments he was away from his farm a lot. In his absence, vandals broke into the place and they were giving the big croc in particular heaps.

'The bastards throw rocks at him, would you believe?' Hilton snorted. 'It'll drive him crazy in the end.'

Intrigued by what Hilton Graham had told him, George decided to check out at first hand his big crocodile. The key word was of course 'big'. George Craig knew all about supposed big crocodiles that, when you finally saw them, almost always failed to measure up.

Not so Hilton Graham's big crocodile. It was truly big. Even allowing for a bit of missing tail, and a slice off his snout, this one had to be nudging 6 metres (19 feet 6 inches) in length. Moreover, he was enormous, built on gargantuan lines. Certainly he was heavier than Oscar — well over a tonne.

So Hilton Graham sold his big crocodile to George Craig and in due course it arrived at Green Island. One pen was exchanged for another. His new home, however, offered a far better lifestyle. No one would throw rocks at him here, not with George Craig regularly prowling around.

More than anything, it was the scars that Cassius carried on his body that interested George. Many were the obvious marks of battle, terrible fights over territory or a female's favours. Same old story we humans know all about.

But it was one scar in particular that really aroused his curiosity: that neat slice off his muzzle. It was much too clean, too surgical-like for another croc to have done it in combat. No, this one had been caused by the crocodile making hard contact with something man-made. The obvious answer — did he even dare to think about it, given Sweetheart's background? — was a propeller!

The story of Sweetheart is well documented. Having said that, it is relevant to present a few facts, because two large crocodiles are involved here.

For approximately five years, that is, 1974–79, a large male crocodile known locally as 'Sweetheart' was responsible for at least 15 attacks causing damage to aluminium dinghies and their outboard motors on a large billabong on the Finniss River in the Northern Territory.

Early in 1979 the pattern of attacks changed and became more frequent. This was a cause for some concern for the safety of participants in a proposed fishing competition on the Sweets Lookout Billabong, even though, rather surprisingly, no one had ever been hurt by Sweetheart.

It was decided to capture Sweetheart alive, to house him in one of the newly established crocodile farms, where he could be used in the breeding programme. His potential to attract visitors would be enormous.

So wildlife rangers from the Conservation Commission were called in to carry out the job of trapping Sweetheart. They did so on the morning of 19 July 1979. Sweetheart's jaws were securely bound, and he was anaesthetised using Flaxedil. Next, he was towed to the boat ramp on the opposite side of the billabong to where he had been captured. But somehow he became tangled on a submerged log, ingested a great deal of water in his drugged state, and consequently drowned.

Sweetheart had the following dimensions:

Total weight	780 kg
Total length	5.1 m
Snout/vent length	2.45 m
Maximum girth	2.3 m
Sex	Male

The stomach contained:
Pig bones and bristles
Two long-necked turtles and
Parts of a large barramundi

The death of the legendary Sweetheart was keenly felt in the Northern Territory; the rangers involved were especially distressed. Sweetheart's untimely death also heralded the end of an era as far as members of the Matngala Weret tribe were concerned. Sweetheart had inhabited a part of their tribal lands, an area they knew as 'Crocodile Dreaming' country. To these Aborigines of the Finniss River Sweetheart was a creature of vast religious significance: he was their totem, a part of their clan, a part of their very being. To many of the tribe, including Nuggett Marjor, Sweetheart was related to them. Therefore, to harm him in any way was to risk the thunder and vengeance of the all-seeing gods.

So how long had Sweetheart lived in the land of the Matngala Weret? A very long time if we are to believe Nuggett Marjor, who was born around 1900. Later, he became a professional crocodile hunter, and was still doing that when hunting came to an end in 1971.

Sweetheart?

'We never had no trouble from that big 'gator,' Nuggett Marjor recalled in much later life. 'We always knew he was there watching us when we went to get turtles or barramundi. But he never go for us. Not even for our dogs. And we never try to shoot or spear him. I saw that big croc lots of times. But he just sat there lookin' at me. He never tried to get me or my dugout canoe. I shot a lot of crocs, but we always left Old Man Sweet's Lookout alone.'

At the time of his death, Sweetheart carried scars around his head, chipped teeth, and a damaged opaque eye. There were also two bullets, flattened lumps of spent lead, in his spine: enough to make any crocodile cranky. How had they got there? A likely explanation is offered by a professional shooter called Ray Petherick who, in 1958, was hunting the Finniss River. More specifically, Sweet's Lagoon, the very heart of Crocodile Dreaming country.

'It was a dark night,' he remembers. 'About nine o'clock, and out of the corner of my eye, I happened to notice a big croc, so I landed the dinghy and sneaked overland to where he was submerged in the shallow water. Suddenly there was this huge splash and he leapt right out of the water, straight at me!

'The bank was only two foot high, but he landed right on top of it in a mountain of spray and tried to knock me into the river. Fortunately for me there were just enough palm trees to stop him from getting to me directly. As soon as I regained myself, I whipped up my rifle and fired. I think I hit him as he rolled back into the water, splashed and writhed about. It had all happened so quickly — one minute he was in the water, and the next six feet away, trying to have a go at me.

'I fired a second time with the .303 and this time I think I hit him in the back — he disappeared beneath the water. While I was looking for him, he surfaced again and charged headlong at our dinghy. Johnny Faulkner was still in it, and he started yelling, then the croc submerged and was gone. We waited around for three days but couldn't see it. Dead ones float to the top after three or four days. I had never known a croc to attack a boat before, at least in the areas I used to shoot.'

So there was very good reason for this particular crocodile, nursing painful wounds, to associate such an aggravation with a small boat. Also, it does seem certain that the crocodile Ray Petherick shot at twice was the same one that the rangers caught in 1979.

It is worth pointing out that at least one more crocodile attack took place in the region of Crocodile Dreaming country in the 1950s. Again a professional shooter was

The exposed roots of mangroves at low tide. A prime spot for crocodiles.

involved. In fact there were two of them in the boat when it happened. They were dead beat, had put in a hard night's work. So they relaxed with a smoke. One of them, with one of his legs dangling over the side of the boat, was wearing rubber (gum) boots. Imagine his surprise when — whump! — a crocodile suddenly grabbed his foot and took off with his rubber boot. Had the man been wearing anything else — a laced-up leather boot, for example — it is quite likely that the crocodile would also have taken what was inside it. As it was, the man suffered only superficial wounds. A good lesson, though.

Also in the same period a local station owner, Max Sargent, had problems with crocodiles taking stock in the same general area. On one occasion they had rounded up a fair-sized herd of horses and left them in a rough yard alongside Sweet's Lagoon. The horses watered there.

Because it was also hot then, they liked to wade out into the water, which was real bad news for the station owner. Later, Max Sargent would recall:

'We lost seventeen horses in five days to those damn crocs and I don't know how many cattle!'

The key word here is 'crocs', which means there was more than one crocodile there capable of killing a horse or cattle beast. That is not normally a small crocodile. So there must have been more than one large crocodile in the lagoon at the time Max Sargent is talking about. On the strength of that, is it not possible that both of the crocodiles under dispute — that is, which of them should truly wear Sweetheart's crown — were involved here?

One puzzling aspect of the whole business is why, if Sweetheart's motives were activated by two bullet wounds, did he wait until 1974 to begin his vendetta? After all, sixteen years is an awfully long time to bear a deep-rooted grudge and do nothing about it.

In all fairness, it must be stressed that once Sweetheart was killed the attacks on boats stopped at Sweet's Lagoon. What does George Craig think about that?

'You know,' he says, 'it would be a real easy mistake to make. Think about it: they set out to catch a big croc at Sweet's Lagoon and they get one, right? They all want it to be Sweetheart, don't they? So Sweetheart it is. It's not as if anyone has really seen him, is it?' George smiled wickedly. 'But maybe — just maybe — the real Sweetheart wasn't caught.'

'Just where was he captured?'

'When I was in Darwin, Graham Webb reckoned it was

about a mile away from where they captured Sweetheart. There was so much activity going on there when they were trying to capture Sweetheart that Cassius could have easily got sick of it and decided to shoot through. It might have suited him better at the other billabong, who knows. I mean, that would explain why there were no more attacks on boats, right?'

A very persuasive fellow, George Craig.

'And there's something else to think on too,' he went on, warming to the subject. 'I've seen Sweetheart up there in Darwin and I don't reckon he's big enough or, for that matter, knocked around enough to have attacked so many boats — was it fifteen?'

'At least that,' I said.

'On the other hand,' George went on, 'Cassius is much heavier than Sweetheart and he's got the right sort of scars to prove it.'

Scars to prove it?

When George lured Cassius out of his pool with a suitable bait, the big one of perhaps ninety years came out of the water with all the energy of a crocodile a third of his age. Even so, I saw how big he was; I also saw his battle-scarred body. Cassius, I thought, might have mixed it with Don Quixote's legendary windmill on a particularly bad day.

'And there's something else,' George continued, 'that backs up my theory …'

On the day he told me about, a Cairns-based hovercraft, on one of its initial runs, had come out to Green Island. The high-level sound it made as it circumnavigated the island was, George says, remarkably like that of an outboard motor at full pitch.

At this time, George was looking after about thirty crocodiles. All but one of them were unmoved by the sound of the hovercraft. The marked exception was — Cassius. The way George tells it, Cassius went right out of his head: he hurled himself around his pen, jack-knifing, working himself into a frenzy.

What did this sound trigger off in Cassius' brain? Did he recall the untold agony of when a propeller had sliced a hunk of his muzzle, or chopped off his arm? Did it bring it all back, sharp and clear, so that for a moment he was back there in Sweet's Lagoon, the jarring sound of an outboard motor coming steadily closer and closer until the compulsion to attack and destroy overwhelmed him?

'So when you think about that,' George finished, 'and weigh up all the other factors, can you blame me for thinking that Cassius is really the rogue croc of Sweet's Lagoon?'

In all honesty I could not.

Naturally, they tend to dismiss such claims in Darwin: Sweetheart is Sweetheart is Sweetheart. End of argument. Even so, there were several people I talked with in Darwin (who wish to remain anonymous) who believe that George Craig has a strong case. Even Hugh Edwards, author of *Crocodile Attack in Australia*, considers it 'very likely' that a mistake has been made.

We will, of course, never know the real story. The problem is that Cassius and, most certainly, Sweetheart will never divulge the truth. The secret will remain where it all happened: in the Crocodile Dreaming country down on the Finniss River.

*Station Country II: Returning to the
New Zealand Back Country* — 1995

A Legend Came This Way

The Darran Mountains, Fiordland National Park.

By any reckoning the wide valley of the Greenstone River was in midsummer very lovely country, and the mobs of Hereford cows and calves only enhanced the picture. The cattle belonged to the Metherell family, who owned Elfin Bay station. The station was once part of Hugh MacKenzie's mighty Walter Peak run.

The Greenstone Valley route from Lake Wakatipu to the West Coast was first used by the Maoris while searching for precious pounamu and hunting moas. The area was rediscovered by Europeans in 1861, when David McKellar and George Gunn headed up the Mararoa River, west of Wakatipu, looking for somewhere to run sheep. They came to the Greenstone Valley and eventually to a beautiful lake, which they named Lake McKellar. Soon they were climbing and became the first Europeans to stand on top of Te Tatau-a-Raki, which they referred to as Key Summit.

In later years this same route would be used by another Gunn — the legendary Davy Gunn — who raised Herefords in the Hollyford Valley. Every year in the late spring he left his beloved West Coast run to take a sizeable herd to Lorneville, out of Invercargill, for the November sales. Gunn's yearly droving trek of more than 300 kilometres, much of it through difficult terrain, took a full three weeks.

It was in 1926 that Davy Gunn, in partnership with William Fraser, purchased the run. The property took in much of the Hollyford Valley and all of the Pyke River, but only about one-tenth of its 60,000 hectares was open country. It was extremely isolated, and the only serious means of access was by sea.

William Fraser soon became disenchanted with the primitive conditions, but Davy Gunn revelled in it all, his keen eyes shining with enthusiasm — within a few years he had bought Fraser out. Slowly he built up his herd of cattle, taking on help when he could afford it. There was no fencing, so the cattle were run semi-wild: the bulls remained with the cows year-round, and the calves were, by and large, self-weaned. By the late 1930s Gunn was running close to 1000 head of cattle and considered the lower Pyke the best country he had.

It was Davy Gunn's droving trips that lifted him to celebrity status in the region. His cattle treks were the stuff of legend, not so much for the distance covered as for the rugged country they traversed. The trips usually involved about 100 head of cattle, the maximum that could be safely handled.

The trek began in Gunn's Lake Alabaster holding yards. Gunn and his men found their way out of the Hollyford Valley via the incredibly steep Deadmans Track, then crossed the Howden Valley, perhaps staying overnight at Lake Howden. The Greenstone Valley was next, followed by the Mararoa Valley. On past the Mavora lakes they went, down the Mararoa, until they reach Mossburn. Trail's end was Lorneville and, with enough cash in his pocket to see him through the year, Gunn wasted no time returning to his run.

Once the Milford road was opened in 1939, Davy Gunn took his cattle via the Eglinton Valley and Te Anau. He was befriended by the Chartres family of Te Anau Downs station; it was here that Colin King first met the legendary Davy Gunn.

By this time Gunn was well into his sixties, a strong man nevertheless, and Colin was not yet twenty-one. Perhaps the older man saw something of himself in the Southland musterer; in any event the two got on well.

Davy Gunn told Colin a story about one of his droving trips. He had been paid for his cattle at Mossburn, from where they would be transported by rail to Invercargill. In

Fallow buck with his thick winter coat. White fallow deer have little or no variation in colour throughout the seasons.

The watershed of the Mavora River.

that somewhere along the way it must have fallen out.

Mounting up, Davy retraced his steps, eyes rarely leaving the ground. Finally he came to the main highway near Mossburn — still no sign of the money. He turned his horse's head about and started back, a year's income lost.

Nearly a year later Davy Gunn's cattle were again yarded in preparation for the yearly trip. Readying his horse for the journey, he picked up the saddle bags and gave them a good shake — and a wad of notes fell out. 'It was,' he later said, 'like getting two incomes in one year!'

By this time, the early to mid-fifties, red deer had invaded Davy Gunn's country from the north. Davy had seen it coming — 'Shoot every one of them you see!' he'd ordered his men — but it was too much for just a few men to handle. Such was the devastation that his 1000 head of cattle had to be reduced to around 400. Davy held grave fears that, lacking winter-feed, some would not make it through the winter. But cattle, like most domesticated stock, are survivors when placed in jeopardy; such were Davy Gunn's semi-wild Herefords.

With his cattle business in decline, Davy stepped up his tourism activities to supplement his income. Huts were built, tracks improved and horses purchased. One of Davy's favourite tourist trips was down the valley of the Hollyford, on to Martins Bay and Big Bay, then back home down the Pyke. Riding in single file below the Darran Mountains, Davy might well have looked up at the towering peaks and recalled one summer day many years earlier.

Davy was up on the tops searching for high-ranging Herefords when, right on the crest of the range, he slipped and plunged headlong into space. Were it not for a narrow ledge some 4 metres below, Davy Gunn would undoubtedly

typical fashion, he returned home quickly, taking four days. Back at the homestead, he put his hand into his trouser pocket to get out the money. Nothing. He always put the tight wad of notes into the same pocket, and he could only deduce

have died. Badly bruised, shocked and in increasing pain, he found himself unable to move. He remained on the ledge as night fell; if for nothing else he was thankful it was summertime.

In the morning one of Davy's men went looking for him, and found a badly shaken Davy still on the ledge. He helped him climb to safety and took him down the mountains to Deadmans hut. 'The mountains nearly got me that time,' he would later say.

Davy Gunn's tourist parties always camped at the hut at Big Bay. They were there on a day Davy would never forget — 30 December 1936.

While he and his clients were on the beach a light aircraft came into sight. It was planning to land on the hard-packed sand, but as it came in something went wrong and the plane crashed. Sutton Jones, a journalist, was killed instantly; the other three passengers were badly injured. Only the pilot escaped serious injury.

Help had to be obtained — fast — and Davy Gunn knew it was all up to him. The nearest telephone was 85 kilometres away, at Marion Camp on the yet to be finished Milford road. Cursing the lack of horse, he set off at a run. It was a slow 25 kilometres to Lake McKerrow and it was nearly dark when he got there.

The track fringing the lake was not called the Demon Trail as a joke; it was tough enough in daylight, let alone at night. Fortunately Davy had a boat moored on the lake and, with a will, he rowed the 20 kilometres to the head of the lake almost non-stop. There was a hut there and Davy paused to make a brew.

Suddenly he heard a whinny. It was one of his free-ranging horses. The lonely animal responded to Davy's soft

Looking across Wakatipu to where the Greenstone River flows into the lake.

call and, saddling up, Davy pressed on into the night.

The following afternoon man and horse arrived at Marion Camp. Davy Gunn, nearly fifty years old, had covered 85 kilometres on foot, in a rowboat and on horseback in twenty-one

Herefords have grazed for a very long time in the valley of the Greenstone.

hours. Stones commemorating his heroism were placed at Marion Camp and in the lower Pyke River.

After leaving Big Bay, Davy's tourist parties would spend a few nights at the huts on the outlying parts of his huge run. From time to time they would run into wild cattle. Real wild cattle, born mean. These scrub bulls would snort and stare defiantly at the intruders — as likely as not the first human beings they had ever seen. Davy would always keep his .303 at the ready, just in case.

Bill Norman, who later farmed in Southland, worked with Davy in 1939 and had several hairy encounters with wild bulls. The most serious happened during the annual muster when, quiet as a cat, a bull confronted them in the thicket-like growth. Davy was on foot.

Bill spotted it first: 'Watch out, Davy!' he warned.

Too late. In an instant the bull was upon him. Thunk! Davy crashed to the ground. The bull could have had him then, for Davy was momentarily stunned. Instead the animal went for Davy's horse. One slashing blow of its deadly horns and the horse's throat was ripped open. Wheeling, the bull then attacked Bill's horse without causing critical injury. The beast raced off, smashing through the tangled undergrowth like a ten-tonne truck. This was tiger country, all right.

On Christmas Day 1955 Davy Gunn, giving seventy years of age a hard nudge, was guiding a three-strong party of tourists. When they came to cross the lower Pyke, Davy put Warren Shaw, at twelve the youngest amongst them, behind him on his own horse.

The Pyke was running faster and dirtier than normal. No matter — this was a regular cattle ford, as safe as houses.

'Hang on, lad,' he laughed as they went in.

Part way across the horse stumbled and fell into a newly scooped hole. Had the river not been running so strong, the horse would have regained its footing in an instant. As it was, it went down on its side, pinning Davy underneath it for a moment. With a mighty effort the horse scrambled to regain its footing, with Davy and Warren clinging to the saddle for dear life. The saddle slipped around the horse's belly and, losing their grip, Davy and the boy were swept away by the current. The rest of the party could only look on in dismay.

Like many a back-country man, Davy Gunn had never learned to swim. Not so the boy, who was considered a good swimmer. In the end it didn't make any difference — the Pyke claimed both lives that Christmas Day.

The news of Davy Gunn's death stunned all who knew him; he had seemed indestructible. But fate, as fickle as the high-country weather, had its own plans for Davy, and in truth it was only right that he should die in the place he had loved for thirty years.

Following the death of his father, Murray Gunn took over the run. A few years later the government included some of the run within the boundaries of Fiordland National Park and ownership was transferred to the Public Trust. There was a muster; it rounded up 360 cattle of which 120 were taken to Lorneville. An attempt was later made to muster the rest, but after two musterers were drowned the Public Trust gave it up as a bad job.

Davy Gunn's cattle would still be there were it not for the helicopter boys. When in the late 1960s the airborne hunters came in for red deer, they also accounted for the several hundred cattle that were the last of Davy's once fine herd.

Lake Howden, Fiordland National Park. Red deer inhabit the forest fringing the lake.

*Holden's New Zealand Venison
Cookbook — 1995*

Frying Pan & Barbecue

*Camp life: no real pressures. Gary Cruickshank is
about to fix a brew and some venison for dinner.*

It was a Saturday in summertime, a little after nightfall. In warm conditions I had set up camp high on the brawny shoulder of the Ngamoko Range, a little-known offshoot of the Ruahine Range. I was on what we government hunters called a flycamp — travelling light and camping out so that you could be on the spot at the two top hunting times, early morning and late evening.

My meal tonight would be a simple but satisfying one, venison steaks. The animal I had taken the meat from was a yearling, the only one of such a tender age in a group of four red deer I'd surprised in a grassy basin just before dark. I'd managed to make a good fire, even at 1500 metres, by breaking up brittle, knotty branches of leatherwood. Fact was, there wasn't anything else you could've made a fire with up there.

Colder now, I yanked on a thick woollen shirt and savoured a mug of black coffee. I mulled over the hunt, wondering what the next morning would bring. After a while I set out on the ground the stuff I'd brought to cook with: a small, light frying pan with a fold-away handle, a big knob of butter and some flour seasoned generously with salt and pepper.

I sliced my Porterhouse steak into thin strips, not because it was easy to do, but because, if it was cooked soon enough, it would make the cooked meat extremely tender. Left for a couple of hours, however, the thin steaks would quickly toughen up. I set the pan on a heap of raked embers, popped in half the lard and, when it was melted and sizzling, added the flour-coated steaks. I cooked them quickly — less than a minute each side — so that the coating was crunchy and meat still a little pink on the inside. That, really, is the secret to grilling or frying venison steaks and chops: don't overdo it. Venison, with its low fat content, doesn't take kindly to being cooked past medium-rare and overcooked venison is tough, dry and tasteless.

I ate my delicious steaks with two thick slices of prebuttered bread and sipped another coffee. Wood smoke drifted across my face and past my rifle and pack. There would be, I mused, enough meat left over for breakfast, even if it was going to be on the tough side by then.

BARBECUE GRILLED VENISON

When you're barbecuing venison steaks, be careful not to cook them over too high a flame or they'll end up charred. Wait until the fire has died down and, in the case of charcoal, a white ash has formed.

Ingredients (serves 4–6)
Marinade

1 c red wine
4 cloves garlic, crushed
2 T safflower oil
2 T olive oil
2 T rosemary
2 bay leaves
pepper

1 kg lean venison, cut into 4–5 cm slices
salt

Method

Combine marinade ingredients, add steaks and allow to stand for 12 hours.

Drain steaks, reserving marinade. Salt steaks liberally, then fry for 2–4 minutes each side on barbecue hot plate in very little oil, basting occasionally with marinade.

Meat in the camp.

Holden's New Zealand Venison
Cookbook — 1995

Mt White coal range.

Two things were obvious when Darryl Steele and I arrived at the old Manson hut on the far eastern fringes of Ngamatea station in the central North Island. First, there was no food cupboard. Second, there was no food to put in a food cupboard. Luckily for us, when we tramped up there that cold autumn day, our backpacks had been loaded down with all the ingredients for a king-sized venison stew.

All too soon, however, the stew was gone and we were back to our old standby of venison steaks cooked in the giant camp oven (roast venison was out of the question because we had run out of fat and oil). True, we could've shot through to one of the Forestry huts to get provisions, but that was a fair hike and we were reluctant to leave the block. The hunting on that side of the Ngaruroro River was so much better, and the rolling, park-like Manson country was a pleasure to stalk. We agreed to see how long we could last on nothing more than venison steaks.

One very wet morning I decided to try and enliven our diet by making jerky, a long, thin strip of dried venison. Now I knew that, on the inland plateau in April, there was no way we could make it the traditional Native American way, by drying it in the sun. But I figured that, seeing as the Inuit (or Eskimo) people also made jerky, it had to be OK to dry it by the heat of a fire. Besides, the wood smoke would impart its own tang to the meat.

Above the huge fireplace at the Manson hut there was an iron bar (as well as criss-crossed number eight wire from which we hung cooking utensils). With a good fire going, I cut several backsteaks into long strips and, salting them well, draped them like wet socks over the bar.

The next day was warm and sunny and Darryl and I set off hunting in different directions, each carrying a dried and shrunken length of Ngamatea jerky. For my part, I found it extremely agreeable to chew on whenever I needed an energy hit. I hunted with rare zest, taking nine reds before I called it quits. Heading back to the hut, I wondered how far you could travel on such power-packed fare. All the way to the Rocky Mountains, I guess.

QUICKFIRE JERKY

An ideal cut for making jerky has a long grain running through it, for example flank steak. The lower grade cuts are a sensible choice. In North America jerky is sometimes stored in the refrigerator in jars with holes punched in the lids, where it will keep for several months. It shouldn't be stored in an airtight container because it will go soft.

Ingredients

700 g lean venison
salt and pepper
2 T Worcestershire sauce
2 T tomato sauce
2 T soy sauce

Method

Once all the fat and gristle is trimmed from the meat, cut it parallel to the grain into strips 15 mm thick and 15 cm long. Sprinkle meat liberally with salt and pepper. Place all ingredients in plastic kitchen bag and mix by gently squeezing. Allow to marinate at room temperature for 5 hours.

Preheat oven to very low, about 70°C. Spray or brush metal rack with cooking oil. Remove meat from bag and pat dry with paper towels. Place on racks in oven, leaving door ajar to allow air to circulate.

Depending on the thickness of the meat, jerky can take anything from 4 to 8 hours to dry. Keep checking the meat — the end product should be shrivelled and cracked, but it should not snap when you bend it.

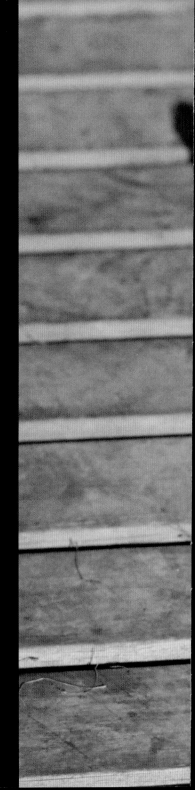

New Zealand Hunter — 1998

Percy Lyes

Boots from a different era. Hunters such as Percy Lyes would have worn these.

F arm manager, timber worker (retired). Born Hokitika, 8 August 1922. Educated Kowhitirangi School. Married Melva Brown, 1960. Three children: Carolyn (1961), David (1962) and Gregory (1966).

Percy first started hunting on the West Coast at the age of 12. He was on the Inaugural Committee of the West Coast branch of the NZDA in 1952, and was an NZDA member for 26 years. In 1955 he won the West Coast single rise clay bird championship. During my now considerable years of reading about hunting in this country, I cannot recall just how many times the name of Percy Lyes has cropped up. Certainly he must rank among the all-time greats in the story of hunting in New Zealand.

Percy Lyes and his brother David started as government hunters in 1947 at Glentanner station. During this season he shot a 13 $^{7}/_{8}$-inch thar scoring 44¾ points. He hunted with Max Curtis (what a combination!) for the season of 1948–49 on the Whitcombe block. They were paid two bob per tail. One day while camped together at Cave Camp they shot 140 deer between them, Max tailing 74 and Percy 66. This must surely be the greatest number of red deer ever taken in a single day by two government hunters operating on foot.

In the tail-end of that season Percy shot a 14-point red stag measuring 50 x 39 inches, still the record for antler 'length' in this country. This magnificent head scores 355 points, placing it in eighth position among the highest-scoring red deer trophies ever taken in this country. He ended that season with 1558 tails to his credit.

Until the advent of high-power rifles and scopes, this was the most commonly used firearm in the country: an open-sighted .303.

Percy would hunt on a number of blocks after that, all on the West Coast. Among his block mates were Tom McDowell, Ivan Jacobs, Bill Davey, and Arthur Curtis. Percy told me a couple of interesting snippets about this time.

In Park Stream of Hokitika 1951 (after wasting most of my ammo on chamois), I found myself with only 26 rounds left and lots of country to cover. I found the deer were sheltering from the wind in the gullies that cut through the tussock slopes. I was able to take my time and line up two or three deer before opening up fire. I got two with one shot twice and three with one shot once.

I once got five deer for one shot on Mount Mitre near the head of the Hokitika. A mob was just disappearing over the skyline in deep snow. When I fired one shot they disappeared — two stag slid down to where I was. When I looked down the other side of the ridge there were three more dead in an icy gully. Whether they were killed by my shot or fell to their death it was too dangerous to find out.

Right from his early days, Percy was fascinated with moose.

I spent the first half of my life eight miles from where moose were first liberated at the Hokitika Gorge. My father used to tell me stories of the cow

Percy Lyes feeding a young thar caught on government control operations, Ben Ohau Range, summer season, 1947–48.

Robin Francis-Smith with moose taken by Percy Lyes, 1952.

moose that used to frequent their camp when he was on the Geological Survey in 1904. One day the cook arrived back at camp to find the back end of a moose protruding from the tent. He gave it a prod with a crowbar and it took off, taking the tent with it.

It was in the April of 1952, in Wet Jacket Arm, that Percy Lyes shot a moose which ranks in second place among the three moose trophies taken in this country. Percy Lyes, who now lives in sunny Taradale, Hawke's Bay, has the distinction of being the only man alive in this country with the antlers of a locally taken bull moose to gaze upon and remember when.

Percy says that he still has his old 1918 .303 rifle. That workhorse of his deer-culling days would have a real story to tell.